THOSE WHO GIVE A DAMN

A Manual for Making a Difference

Those Who Give A Damn is a non-fiction book based on the author's experiences, challenges and triumphs.

All Rights Reserved ©2018 Duvalier J. Malone

The editorial arrangement, analysis, and professional commentary are subject to this copyright notice. No portion of this book may be copied, retransmitted, reposted, duplicated, or otherwise used without the express written approval of the author, except by reviewers who may quote brief excerpts in connection with a review.

United States laws and regulations are public domain and not subject to copyright. Any unauthorized copying, reproduction, translation, or distribution of any part of this material without permission by the author is prohibited and against the law.

Disclaimer and Terms of Use: Your reliance upon information and content obtained by you at or through this publication is solely at your own risk. The author assumes no liability or responsibility for damage or injury to you, other persons, or property arising from any use of any product, information, idea, or instruction contained in the content or services provided to you through this book. Reliance upon information contained in this material is solely at the reader's own risk.

ISBN-13: 978-1986148306

ISBN-10: 1986148300

Front Cover Photo by Tenola Plaxico • Author Photo by Bouvier Ellis

Edited by: Theatrical Harmony Media

Cover and interior design by Rebecca Shaw, BrockleyDesigns.com

THOSE WHO GIVE A DAMN

A Manual for Making a Difference

DUVALIER J. MALONE

Dedication

Thank you to my mother for instilling faith, courage, and the ability to rise above adverse circumstances.

To my life partner, Adrian, thank you for helping me discover my authentic truth.

And thank you, the future change maker for using your voice and truth to initiate change in the world.

Introduction

How a small town boy dreamed of changing his fate. You may know his story, but do you understand his struggle?

Those Who Give A Damn is a story of struggle, adversity and the will to succeed. Join Duvalier Malone as he details how he overcame tragedy in the best way possible: in the service of his fellow man and woman.

Duvalier seeks to give a manual on how to serve humanity. As a small town boy who chased his dreams and found the path to manhood that was forged by the footsteps of those who paved the way, Duvalier was blessed with the tools to give back to his community.

He now wants to share those tools with others, by showing through example how to rise above one's circumstances and achieve in spite of the hardships and obstacles that lay in one's way.

While agonizing over his own place in the world, Duvalier discovered that his measure was hidden in his own courage, strength and hope. This moment of achievement is chronicled in the memoir of this community servant who wishes to inspire others the way he was inspired by those who went before him.

Chapter Overview

Chapter 1: An introduction to Duvalier's life and the important figures who guided him during his early years. Duvalier describes the monumental moments that set him on his current path, such as his trip to Washington DC where he met his Congressional representatives.

Chapter 2: This part of the story chronicles Duvalier's early adulthood, and how he began to use his platform to galvanize the community, inspiring them to seek a seat at the table, and hold their elected officials responsible for the state of the community.

Chapter 3: Duvalier realizes that while he has inspired others to lay responsibility at the feet of elected officials, that he is not immune to the same criticisms. This is where there's a marked change in his written columns and speeches at events. Duvalier understands that he too has been given a platform; and he is equally as responsible to use his platform to create the change that he has championed.

Chapter 4: After much reflection, Duvalier decides to lend his voice to a dangerous movement: The fight against racism and hatred. He puts much on the line by speaking boldly, challenging the governor of Mississippi to denounce the racist history of the state. Duvalier stands at the forefront of the movement to remove the Confederate symbol from the Mississippi state flag.

Chapter 5: As he moves onto the national stage with published columns in USA Today, Duvalier begins to address issues that affect minorities across the country. He becomes a warrior in the fight against racism, and he uses his voice to demand justice for the 1955 murder of Emmett Till.

Chapter 6: After the historic presidency of Barack Obama, Duvalier is left to wonder: What's next? He tackles this question head-on, while remaining hopeful; but he is also forced to consider the presidency of Donald Trump, and what this means for the future of America.

Chapter 7: For 30 years, Duvalier spent his life not standing in his complete truth. He allowed his Southern roots along with public opinion to cultivate his truth instead of finding his own voice. By standing in his truth, he found his voice.

Table of Contents

Dedication v

Introduction vii

Chapter Overview 9

Chapter 1 My Journey to Service 13

Chapter 2 Rural Reach 55

Chapter 3 Our Seat at the Table 79

Chapter 4 Symbols of Hate 105

Chapter 5 Confronting Issues Across the Nation 133

Chapter 6 The President That Gave Us Hope 161

Chapter 7 My Truth Gave Me My Voice 185

About the Author 191

Chapter 1

My Journey to Service

I want to tell you my story about how I became an activist and community leader, and why I decided to dedicate my life to being a change agent.

But of course, all stories must start at the beginning. After all, our past is what drives our present, and motivates our decisions that advance our future.

My story begins in the small community of Harriston, Mississippi, where I was born and raised. Harriston lies just outside the town of Fayette in Jefferson County. Fayette has great historical significance, as the town that elected Mr Charles Evers as the first black mayor in the South since Reconstruction.

I believe that this rich historical region is what helped to shape my political views. But although Jefferson County had such noted history and background, it was known as one of the poorest counties in Mississippi and the entire country.

That's where my story begins – in poverty. Growing up, my family battled a lot of issues. Being born into a family that was less than fortunate was a huge setback for my siblings and me.

But I think that's what helped to instill in us the drive to succeed. You see, having that obstacle of poverty forced me to dream of a successful future. I knew that I didn't want to spend my life living like this. I knew that I wanted to do something that would help my entire family.

So I dreamed. I dreamed of my family in a better house, a better neighborhood and a better environment.

But the driving force behind these dreams was the sad reality of my childhood. My family experienced dark days, some that I still hesitate to speak on. But I want to share my story with you because there are those who are going through what I went through, and it's important that you know that there's a light at the end of the tunnel.

Up until I was 12 years old, both my parents were in our home. But due to my father's deteriorating mental state, our family started to experience extreme hardship.

My father's mental illness wreaked havoc on our family. Not only did it affect his relationship with my mother, but it also negatively impacted the dynamic of our household. My school performance even began to suffer.

One day, my father came to us and told us that he no longer wanted a family – and he left.

That hit us like a ton of bricks. I didn't know what to think. The only thing I could think was, "What are we going to do?"

Up until that time, my mother was a stay-at-home mom. So when my father decided that he wanted a divorce, it was devastating to us both morally and financially.

We lived on my father's family land, and it was the only life I had known. My father moved next door to my grandmother's house as they went through the divorce process, but even though he was so close, he wanted nothing more to do with us.

My siblings and I were now in a single-parent home. Neither our mother nor we could understand why my father had chosen to throw his family away, leaving us in confusion, hopelessness, and loss.

We had no help. Once my father left, the rest of his siblings wanted nothing to do with us. My father and his siblings decided that they no longer wanted us on the family land.

So here we were, in terrible straits, not even knowing where our next meal would come from. My mother would often pray to God to heal my father's mind and bring him back home, and at the same time, she would pray that God would allow us to have food on the table so that we could survive.

She relied on her faith. I remember one specific moment when we were completely out of food, and my mother began to pray and say, "God is going to provide for us, and I guarantee you that we'll have food when you guys get out of school."

I didn't believe her. At that point in my life, I had been through so much where I didn't expect anything good to happen. I only expected the worst. And when I got home, there still was no food on the table.

But my mother reminded us of her promise, and she assured us that God would provide. And later that day, one of my mother's friends brought over a box of food.

That was one of our better days, knowing that we had enough food to sustain us for the next week and a half. And this is what showed me what it meant to stand and believe God for the impossible.

I know that many are dealing with poverty and debt. There are those who are trying to raise their child in a single parent home with limited income. You're trying to raise your family to strive for the achievements that lie ahead.

But the moral of my story is that whenever you are in need, just remember that God is watching over every one of us. He provides our needs. I remember always hearing older people say that the Lord may not come when you want him to, but He's always on time.

I'm telling my story now because I've seen so many who were beaten down and robbed of their faith through circumstances that were out of their control. The hardships that they faced in their lives impacted them to the point where they no longer wanted to attend church and believe in that higher being.

Well, I can only speak for my life, but I believe it was my family's faith that helped to pull us out of our situations.

No, I'm not telling you that it happened overnight. We continued to struggle. I vividly remember waiting anxiously every month for my mother's government assistance to come in, and cross my fingers and hoping that the food would be enough for the entire month.

There were times when I had to go to my father and tell him that we were hungry. He would always tell me that I could eat there, but don't take anything back to the house.

Of course, I didn't listen. I knew that my father's mental illness often clouded his judgment; and I am still convinced today that if he wasn't sick, that he would have been there for us. So I would do what I knew was right: I would go into my father's refrigerator and pack my book bag with food to feed our family.

Mental illness is a real issue that impacts millions of Americans. Since I spent my life being affected by this tragic circumstance, I feel that it's only right to use my story to encourage others. I want you to know that there is a light at the end of the tunnel, and things will get better.

It may sound like a cliché right now, but life truly does get better, and the sunlight always comes out after the darkness.

I was able to attach to a dream at a young age, which gave me something to reach for during my darkest times. Even while my mother dealt with a terrible situation, she still played a large hand in shaping my future in public service.

This shaping process started at an early age. I was seven when I first dreamed of working in politics. I imagined myself on the political stage as I watched C-SPAN and other local news stations.

I was a curious little boy.

I'm sure it was puzzling to my family when I preferred listening to "Let's Talk", the radio show by Mr Charles Evers, instead of going outside and playing as other children did. But little did my family know that even at that young age, I was in awe and admiration of Mr Evers, and I had made the decision that I wanted to do what he did.

I wanted to be a part of the political and intellectual discourse in my community.

As I listened to Mr Evers' show, I began to feel more connected to the Civil Rights struggle of my parents, grandparents, and ancestors. Mr Evers himself was a bastion of this movement, and through him, I relived the struggle for equality.

When he described the various political, social and economic hurdles that we had to climb, it was my connection to the past: He served in the place of an ancestor passing down stories about the mountain of struggles that his generation had to navigate to survive.

When Mr Evers talked about the March on Washington as well as the local marches within the community, I felt as if I was right there with them as they marched for social changes that resulted in the freedoms that we have today.

♦ ♦ ♦

Mr Evers mentored me through his radio show. As he discussed local and state government and his efforts to lobby for funding to improve our community's water system as well as housing and healthcare, his voice gave me a unique sense of hope.

As I continued to listen, I gained a sense of awareness; and I began to realize that I could rise above the obstacles that were set before me.

During this tender period, I gained perspective from other influences, most notably my grandmother, the late Mary Malone. My grandmother was a part of the Civil Rights movement to gain equality and justice in Mississippi.

She guided me as I began to buck against the norm, and reach for something beyond myself. At that point in time, I didn't know what I was reaching for, but I like to think that my grandmother knew it even before I did.

Although she only received an 11th-grade education, my grandmother was known for her ability to write and speak well; and she began to educate me in the art of public speaking and writing.

As I look back now, I believe that she saw my future. She unarguably trained me in the two most valuable skills that I still greatly rely on to this day.

My grandmother was a pillar of the community. She served her church, and through her, I found my roots in God.

She taught me to speak at Easter programs, Usher board meetings, the Church Founder's Day program, and Vacation Bible School.

She placed me in charge of the Usher Board program and the Youth Auxiliary conference. My tasks were to organize, plan and orchestrate media outreach for church events.

It seemed that my grandmother wanted me to find my roots in God just as my mother did so that I wouldn't grow disillusioned with the world.

At the time, I didn't understand why she made me attend so many events, as well as speak and recite poetry. But as I grew and began to see my dreams unfold before me, I understood what my grandmother saw. She prepared me for my career in public service.

While she guided me to spiritual awareness, my grandmother also took great pains to educate me on civic matters. She would sit me down and tell me stories of how the African American community struggled for the right to vote, the right to sit in public restaurants and the right to sit at the front of the bus.

These stories began to hit home for me as I faced injustices.

But at the time, I began to get a taste of the power that lied within me, that lies within each of us.

My talents were unfolding. I found that I had the ability to speak to people and to influence positive change and make a difference in my community.

This revelation compelled me to research local political activists. As I began to see where my path would lead me, I desired to learn more. The activists that I met encouraged me on my path. They taught me the craft, how to build my brand, how to research my area of interest and how to target the population.

As I soaked in their knowledge and experiences, I could feel that I was being led to something. I just didn't know what.

At the age of 16, I experienced what was perhaps the most important milestone in my life. I feel that this was the age where my purpose really began to unfold.

It started when my grandmother approached me with an idea.

She saw an advertisement for an essay contest that was being sponsored by the Southwest Electric Power Association (SEPA).

The prize for winning the essay contest was an all-expenses-paid trip to Jackson, the State Capital of Mississippi, and a trip to Washington, DC.

My grandmother encouraged me to compete. She was extremely confident in my writing ability, and she told me that I could win.

I will never forget the title of the essay: "How would you use your community influence to make a positive change?"

The title hit me because this topic was something that I had been thinking about for a while. It was as if those days spent listening to my grandmother, and to Charles Evers, while trying to escape the reality of my family's domestic life, had prepared me to answer a question that perhaps most teenagers weren't equipped to answer.

I often say that this is an example of bad circumstances empowering an individual to succeed in future endeavors.

So that day, I started on my essay; and I was able to finish it in only a few hours.

After my grandmother reviewed it and gave me her blessing, I decided to take it to school the next day so that my English teacher, Ms Nekeisha Ellis, could proofread and give me pointers.

Ms Ellis was excited to discover that I was able to use this outlet to plan my future. She was aware of my hardships at home, as it had affected my grades at various points in life. She felt that this contest was the perfect distraction from my home situation, as well as the perfect opportunity to talk about my ideas of working within the community to affect positive change for the betterment of all humanity.

She gave me positive feedback on the essay. She showed me how to improve my thoughts and ideas. As I rewrote the essay, my anticipation grew with every period that I placed at the end of a sentence.

I finished the corrections in minutes because I was so excited and anxious to enter the essay into the contest. I took the revised essay back to my grandmother so that she could re-read it and give her feedback.

To this day, I remember her exact words. In her still, small voice, she told me, "Grandson, you can do whatever you put your mind to, and this essay is a product of that."

After I received my grandmother's blessing and approval, I prepared to submit my essay the next day.

At school, so many other students were also participating in the contest, and they submitted their essays to the school. But I had built so much anticipation and excitement that I just couldn't drop my essay off to my teachers as the other students were doing.

I wanted to personally place my essay in the hands of the chairperson of the SEPA committee.

So I called my mother from school and asked her to pick me up early. When she came, I got in her car with a feeling of elation. I knew that this could be the opportunity to change my life forever.

We arrived at SEPA at around 2 PM that day. I walked in and boldly asked the receptionist, "Who should I speak with regarding the Youth Leadership Essay?"

She replied, "You can drop it off here at the front desk if you like, or you can drop it off to the Chair of the Committee, Mrs Azelda Knight."

Of course, I wanted to meet the Chair and hand-deliver my essay to her. So the receptionist called the Chair's extension, and Mrs Knight came to the front desk.

I introduced myself and shook her hand firmly, as I proudly handed my essay to her. I remember what I told her: "This is my completed essay for the Youth Leadership Council, and I look forward to going to the State and the Nation's Capital with you guys."

Mrs Knight responded with a huge smile, and told me, "I love your confidence, and I am excited about reading your essay."

As my mother and I left SEPA, I was overcome with an excited sense of anxiety. It was over. I wrote my essay, turned it in, and now everything was out of my hands. All I could do now was wait.

Days passed, and I didn't hear anything. I wondered if SEPA had chosen a different student. Even though I put my all into it, maybe my essay just wasn't good enough.

Exactly a week later (on Friday), I said a quick prayer as I got up from my bed that morning: "Lord, if it is your will for me to be a community leader, please allow me the opportunity to win this contest. Please give me the opportunity to see and experience this with my own eyes."

I felt that I had been watching political discourse and community involvement on television and listening to it on the radio for so many years, that now would be the moment where I would either get thrust into it or realize that perhaps my path would lead me in a different direction.

After I said my prayer, I got ready for school and caught the bus as I had done so many mornings before. On the bus ride, the anticipation began to torment me. Feelings of doubt tore at my mind, and I couldn't help but feel despair and the lingering feeling of, "Maybe I just wasn't good enough."

You see, coming from a broken household, it was easy to have feelings of self-doubt. My mother and grandmother did all they could to encourage me, but without my father around, there was just something missing; and without it, I often was plagued by a lack of confidence.

What was normally a 20-minute bus ride to school seemed to last an eternity that morning, as these thoughts roiled through my mind.

When the bus finally pulled into my high school parking lot, I made my way to the front of the bus. But before

I could even get off, Mrs Hill, a high school outreach counselor and parent coordinator, ran to me. She told me, "Duvalier, meet me after breakfast so that I can take pictures of you to put in the local newspaper because YOU'RE THE WINNER OF THE SOUTHWEST EPA ESSAY CONTEST!"

The feelings of anticipation and doubt melted away immediately as I became completely thrilled and overwhelmed with joy. The rest of the school day was almost a blur because my mind was abuzz with excitement. I'm sure I walked around that day with nothing but a huge smile plastered on my face.

My friends at school, who knew about my interest in government and political affairs, were as excited as I was. As I walked into Ms Ellis' classroom, I eagerly announced the happy news that I had just received. But as I struggled to get the words out because of the overwhelming emotion of joy, she knew it. She could see in my eyes that I was at the start of the journey of my life.

I credit Ms Ellis with explaining the importance of this opportunity. She encouraged me to prepare myself by reading the Constitution of the United States and by studying various Presidents so that I would be well-prepared for the conversation on various topics and discussions during the leadership forum.

When it was time to prepare for the trip to Jackson, Southwest EPA chairwoman Azelda Knight scheduled a meeting with my mother and me to discuss the logistics of the trip. Of course, I was bubbling with excitement.

When we walked into Mrs Knight's office, she warmly welcomed us with a huge smile, and she showed my mother the paperwork that we would need to sign. The paperwork consisted of agreements that would secure my place on the trip to Jackson, MS in March and to Washington, DC that following July.

Mrs Knight proceeded to tell me, "Duvalier, after reading your essay, the committee unanimously decided that you were the perfect fit for the youth leadership council."

She leaned closer and joked with me, "You told me when you dropped off your essay that you would see me at the State and the Nation's Capital, and indeed, you are going."

My mother and I listened as Mrs Knight began to explain the process of the trips. I would be spending a week in Jackson, and a week in Washington, DC.

The trip to Jackson would consist of: a tour of the State Capital, a meeting with local members of Congress and State senators from various districts, and a leadership summit that would host numerous guest speakers such as

Amy Tuck, Ronnie Musgrove, Mayor Frank Melton, Senator Thad Cochran and Senator Trent Lott.

After she made sure that we understood everything that would be involved, Mrs Knight proceeded to tell us about the trip to Washington DC. This trip would include an all-expenses-paid flight to Washington, a tour of the city, a tour of the White House, and meetings with two members of Congress from my congressional district: Congressman Bennie Thompson and Congressman Chip Pickering.

So there we were a single mother and her teenage son preparing for something that we could never have foreseen. I knew that I would have the opportunity to experience my dreams, but I could never have imagined that it would come so soon.

When my mother and I left the Southwest EPA building, I was in a daze. I was so excited that I was numb. I still couldn't believe that this was happening. It was completely surreal.

When we went to my grandmother's house, I remember telling her, "Grandmother, I cannot believe that I'm actually going to experience what I've been dreaming about my entire life."

She warmly replied, "This is your season."

I replayed her words many times in my head then, and many times since then. I think that was what convinced me to just embrace the moment. I had been in constant reflection over this blessing that had been set before me. But my grandmother's words stuck with me, and I decided to savor every moment of this milestone in my life.

As someone that came from poverty, this opportunity was it for me. There are many families that are well-off, and they are able to travel and let their children experience the beauty of this country.

But my family wasn't able to give me those kinds of opportunities. Looking back now, I'm glad that it all worked out this way. It gave me a greater appreciation and love for those who come from the background of poverty and inequality. And this is what has driven me to give others the opportunity to have the same experiences that I did.

After all, this is what changed my life. I feel that I have to do what I can to change the lives of others.

The opportunity to help others was what I had prayed for so many times during my youth.

Before I knew it, it was time. I had planned for so long, and now my visit to the State's Capital was hanging right in front of me.

It's amazing how well I remember this day. I guess I shouldn't be surprised. I can credit this trip with giving me my first glimpse into the life of public service, and what happens behind the scenes.

My mother helped me prepare the day of my trip. After I was ready, she took me to the Southwest EPA building in Lorman, MS, and then Mrs Azelda Knight and I set out to Jackson.

This wasn't my first time in Jackson, but this was my first time going with such intent and purpose. This made the city almost brand new for me.

When we arrived at the Crown Plaza Hotel in downtown Jackson, I remember thinking, "Oh wow! I'm in the State Capital!"

As we were checking in, I saw many other students from across the State. It was exciting. I started to wonder about all these new faces, eager to share thoughts and exchange ideas with my fellow student leaders.

I thought to myself, "This must be what revolution looks like!"

Being surrounded by fellow student leaders who were collectively inspired by the same common goals was inspiring. But this was just the beginning.

I registered that afternoon, and soon I found myself shaking hands with then-mayor of Jackson, Frank Melton. It was unbelievable and tremendously humbling at the same time to meet one of the political leaders that I watched and admired during my youth. I had often seen Mayor Melton on television, and I drew so much inspiration from his courageous spirit.

Then the conference began. I was almost overwhelmed. There were so many different seminars to choose from. They included healthcare exchange, social issues, human rights forums, educational symposiums, and open-floor concept meetings on poverty and economic development.

I didn't know which forum to choose first! But after much consideration, I decided to choose something that was close to my heart. My primary platform during my high school years was centered around mobilizing students intellectually. And so I decided on the "Education in the State of Mississippi" symposium.

I had always believed that education could help break the cycle of poverty. While attending the education forum, I experienced an awakening moment. I realized that I, like so many others, had been taking my education for granted.

As the forum speaker went through the importance of education, I was able to understand that I had been living an average academic life, only doing the bare minimum to succeed.

Because I hadn't previously considered the power of academic excellence, I engaged in basic rudimentary actions just to pass from one grade to the next.

So here I was, with this incredible dream of doing great things within my community and across the country, and I realized even more that I had been taking my education for granted.

This was when I decided to get serious about my academics.

As the speaker began to cover the importance of the ACT, the SAT, and even internships, I started to think about the work that I would need to do to develop a formidable academic pedigree.

This inspired me to draft a list of goals. I knew that in order to take my life in the direction that I wanted to go, I would need to develop and focus myself.

I had a short time-frame if I wanted to improve myself academically before high school was over drastically. So I added to the list periodically throughout the seminar.

As the list grew, I could see my line-of-sight focusing and narrowing in on the most important goals. They were to get a good score on the ACT, make a list of colleges and universities that I would like to attend, make a list of careers that I could see myself in, improve my grades, and work adamantly to grow and diversify my group of mentors and professional influences.

When the education seminar was over, we took a break. This gave me time to sit back and truly reflect over my academic career. Now that I knew what my goals were, I would have to create formative change in my life to align myself with those goals.

It was sobering to realize that while my goals and ambitions glittered with enthusiasm, my scholarship did not. It was at that very moment that my focus shifted. No longer was I singularly focused on my future political career. I decided that I would have to equally cultivate my academic career if I was ever to have the political future that I envisioned.

So I began to plan. How could I improve my GPA so that I could have the greatest chance of attending an excellent university? These were the types of questions that were foremost in my mind.

And this is why I credit this educational seminar for prompting a transformative shift in my dreams, goals, and ambitions.

Throughout my entire week at the leadership summit, I felt my horizons expand. I heard so many great stories from local political leaders as they discussed their victories, and also their struggles.

I realized that their backgrounds were not dissimilar to mine as they talked about their origins and how some of them were born and raised in small, poverty-stricken communities.

After I heard all the speakers, I began to realize that what my grandmother always told me was true. She would routinely look at me, and say, "Duvalier, he who thinks he can, can."

When I left Jackson, Mississippi, I left with newfound confidence and the ability to plan for my future.

It was strange. I felt that the leadership conference gave me wings, and yet it also grounded me. I began to realize that it was not all about me.

For the first time in my life, I felt a profound sense of purpose and responsibility. I realized that it was my life's goal and challenge to wield my gifts and opportunities into tangible, effective changes for my community.

The scope by which I could affect people extended beyond the parameters of my family, my community, and church.

The only limits I had were the ones that I had imagined for myself, and I began to realize that they weren't real. I decided that I would work tirelessly to use my assets to affect change.

Being back home gave me a breather period that allowed me to reflect on everything that had happened. It was then that I saw that this was a divine moment that God had created uniquely for me.

When I went back to school, my high school academic counselor Mrs Brown was waiting to take pictures and get my story of how the journey to Jackson, MS changed my life.

I surprised her by asking for a copy of my high school transcripts. After taking a look at the classes I had taken, I told her about all the times that I merely sat in class, but didn't necessarily give my all or interact engagingly. I told her how I could see now that I had been taking my academics for granted.

"How did you come to this conclusion?" she asked me, astounded by the new change that had come over me.

I told her, "Mrs Brown, during my journey to Jackson, I met students from all over the State of Mississippi who had traveled to Washington DC, who were paid scholars and whose ACT scores were 25 and above. The average GPA for all the students who attended the convention was a 3.5 on a 4.0 scale, and they would all have summer internships after returning from Washington, DC."

Mrs Brown nodded in affirmation as I told her of my new purpose to improve my academic status in high school.

She replied and told me, "I really wish we had the resources to send more students off to have such an awakening moment as you have had."

I remember thinking to myself at that moment, "One day, I will have the resources and the opportunities to give back to my community, and help other students to realize their potential as I now realize mine."

That conversation with Mrs Brown reaffirmed my calling as a community activist.

As I left Mrs Brown and walked down the halls of my high school, my fellow students were so excited to see that I was home from my week-long trip to Jackson.

They were abuzz with questions.

"How was it?"

"Who did you meet?"

There were so many questions. They wanted to see pictures and hear the details of my experience.

So many students had taken an interest in my trip, that my Social Studies teacher allowed me to do a presentation on my quest to Jackson, and my upcoming trip to Washington, DC.

Looking back now, I can see that this was my first moment where I helped students to realize their potential. Hearing stories from my travels encouraged my fellow classmates to dream beyond the constraints of their adversity, and to take their scholastic obligations more seriously.

That was my focus during my presentation: How can I relate to my fellow classmates the endless possibilities that the world had to offer? I wanted to get them to understand that we were not a product of our community. We were the answer to our community.

And so I encouraged them as best I could. I told them my thoughts, about how poverty and hardships were nothing but stepping stones that would help position each of us for an even greater level of success.

At the conclusion of my presentation, I asked each of my classmates to make a list: I told them to write down their goals and objectives after our high school graduation. Then I told them to make another list: To write down how they planned to attain those goals and aspirations.

I desired to share the lessons that I had learned from my trip to Jackson. I had learned something very important regarding my future success, and I wanted to pass it on.

While talking with the other students my age, I could speak with enthusiasm regarding the dreams I had for my future and my plans once I achieved success. However, what I could not do was fashion a concrete outline for the ways I planned to achieve that success.

I know this is a problem for many young people that are in the infancy of their creativeness and professional careers. It's like, you can see the apex of the mountain, but you have no conceivable plan for how to navigate the steep inclines or endure the harsh conditions of the terrain.

Coming back from Jackson, I understood that my upbringing and schooling had taught me to dream big, but had not yet taught me how to attain those goals.

There were many students at the leadership conference who had dreams as big as mine.

Some dreamed of becoming a doctor or a lawyer or a politician or an actor. Some even had hopes of becoming the President of the United States.

When asked questions like, "How are you going to attain these goals?, What are your plans?, What have you already been doing to make these goals attainable?", the majority of them were able to articulate their goals, plans and objectives, and the ways that they had planned to achieve those goals.

Listening to them was astounding to me. These were young mavericks who not only had larger-than-life dreams, but they were even equipped with a solid plan of action.

This was why I felt it was so vital that I share with my classmates (and other impressionable youth) the importance of having hopes, but also having an action plan to activate those hopes.

After all, a dream without a plan is just a wish.

Then it came to me: The vision for a youth-oriented foundation. I would call it, "Dream to Succeed."

Right then and there, I made a promise to myself that when I had the necessary tools, I would fund a program designed specifically to afford young people from rural communities the opportunity to be exposed to broader horizons and educate and mentor to attain their goals and aspirations.

But even with this awakening experience, I was still nervous about my impending trip to the Nation's Capital.

Even though I had such a successful trip to Jackson, I remember feeling conflicted while preparing for my journey to Washington, DC. I felt feelings of great excitement, and also lingering sentiments of nervousness and doubt. I was apprehensive.

This was to be my very first trip out of the State of Mississippi.

Going to Jackson was one thing. I was familiar with the city and the region. But Washington, DC was a whole other matter entirely.

I was about to experience so many firsts. It was my very first flight and trip to DC.

The night before the trip as my mother helped me pack and prepare, I remember thinking, "Oh my God, I pray I don't get sick on the plane, and I hope people can't tell that I've never flown before!"

My Journey to Service

When my mother and I left home, the closer we got to the airport, the more nervous I became. But then I started to remember something that my grandmother always taught me. She told me that when you go places, even if you've never been there before, act as if you've already been there.

So by the time I headed to the checkpoint in the airport to meet the other students, I was calm and relaxed. Because I was so confident as we prepared to board the plane, all the other students figured that I had been riding airplanes my entire life.

The flight was calm and soothing. But as I flew into Washington, DC for the very first time, I was almost overcome with emotion. Seeing the Nation's Capital with my own eyes was the moment where I witnessed my lofty childhood dreams starting to become a dazzling reality. I thought to myself, "Dreams really do come true."

As the plane landed, I began to prepare myself for the entire week of tours, seminars, symposiums, workshops and panel discussions.

I looked over the agenda for the week. As I scanned the various events, I was particularly thrilled about the visit to Capitol Hill to meet my local congressmen, Congressman Bennie Thompson and Congressman Chip Pickering. I was also excited about the tour of the White House.

On the day that I met with the Congressional representatives, I struggled to hide how elated and nervous I was.

I remember nervously contemplating which suit I should wear, as I rehearsed the various ways I might introduce myself that would be both appropriate and impressive.

I finally chose a suit, basing my clothing choice on the politicians that I often saw on television. I figured that if I dressed like them, I couldn't go wrong.

So I settled on a blue suit, white shirt and a red tie. Classic.

While I was still preparing that morning, Mrs Knight arrived with some good news. Not only would we be able to meet our local congressmen, but we would also be able to take photographs with our local senators.

I remember being extremely excited because I had heard so much about Senator Thad Cochran and Senator Trent Lott.

When we arrived at the Hill, our first stop was the Senator's offices. I met both senators, and I also took photos with them and got their autographs.

I remember being so overwhelmed at the moment because this was the moment that I had dreamed about for so long.

I was further surprised because the senators themselves opted to take the students on a tour. They even took us inside the chamber where important political decisions were made, and we were able to sit in on one of the legislative sessions.

I thought to myself: "This truly is the dream of every young person who aspires to work in government."

This made me appreciate the moment even more. I realized that there were so many that had never been given the opportunity to sit where I now sat and see and hear the things that I was now hearing.

After we left the senators, we proceeded to meet our two local congressmen. Sitting down with Congressman Chip Pickering and Congressman Bennie Thompson was an incredible experience.

The students were given ten minutes with each congressman from our district. I introduced myself to Congressman Chip Pickering first, telling him where I was from and what I wanted to do after school. I explained my plans to attend college, major in political science; and then I told him that one day, I hoped to work within my community and make a difference.

I remember Congressman Pickering's response like it was yesterday. He told me, "There's something special about you."

The next step was Congressman Bennie Thompson's office. I was somewhat familiar with him already. I had seen his commercials and heard some of his speeches. I even attended some of his campaign fundraising events in Fayette.

But although I had these minor brushes with him, I never had the opportunity to meet Congressman Thompson and have a discussion with him.

As we walked into his office, I wondered what I would find. Then fortune struck. I saw a familiar face – my first cousin, Jamie Sturgis.

As it turns out, she was interning for the congressman while she was attending graduate school at Carnegie Mellon. She and I weren't particularly close; but still, being from our small town and having the opportunity to run into someone that we knew in this big city was a great experience for us both.

I hadn't seen Jamie since our family reunion. She excitedly introduced me to the other staff members as I waited for the meeting with Congressman Thompson.

Seeing her helped to eliminate the last vestiges of anxiety that had consumed me just moments before. For the next few minutes, through virtue of my cousin, she and the rest of the interns and staff members began to share their experiences with us.

It was incredible, hearing these stories from people whose backgrounds were not so dissimilar from my own; and in the case of my cousin, very similar to mine.

The rest of the students and I were able to sit with them for maybe 15 minutes before Congressman Thompson's assistant came out to notify us that he was ready to meet with us.

Even though seeing my cousin quieted the nervousness in my belly, it all came rushing back to the realization that this was it. Now my anxiety was worse than before. I felt a sinking in the pit of my stomach, and even a trembling sensation in my heart.

What was I afraid of? Disappointment? Not Congressman Thompson disappointing me, of course. Here I was a poor boy from a small community in Mississippi. Congressman

Thompson was a larger-than-life figure to me, a teenager that visited his office in 2001.

He couldn't disappoint me if he tried. I wasn't aware enough to know his political positions, and I wasn't conscious enough to be able to decide if I agreed with them, even I had known them.

No, I wasn't afraid of Congressman Thompson being a disappointment to me. I was afraid of being a disappointment to him.

What if I said the wrong thing? What if heading into his office with this group of exceptional students showed that there was nothing exceptional about me?

I was afraid that I would be shown to be the least deserving of all of them. Maybe I didn't belong here.

To me, this moment was as monumental as meeting a celebrity. I felt this added pressure with Congressman Thompson as opposed to Congressman Pickering. Why?

Perhaps it was because Congressman Thompson was a representative for me and the struggles that I was always told of. He was from my home. Not just my state, but the same area, the same struggles that I was faced with.

This is what he represented to me.

When I shook the congressman's hand, it was as if a jolt of lightning coursed through me. After I introduced myself, I stepped back to allow the other students room to get close to him and shake his hand.

I wondered to myself if they felt the same as I did. Most of them smiled politely and seemed excited, but I wondered if they were faced with the same feelings of anxiety and excitement as I was.

As they greeted the congressman, I decided to take a moment to look around his office. I was surrounded by walls filled with records of his accomplishments. His accolades seemed to decorate every space in the room.

I saw awards from numerous community-based organizations such as The Urban League, the NAACP, the National Democratic Party and the Congressional Black Caucus.

Something inside me compelled me to make mental notes of these organizations so that I could research them when I returned home. As the other students busied themselves with meeting the Congressman, my mind buzzed with thoughts. "What is a caucus? What does the Urban League do?" I didn't want to let any information from this trip go to waste.

But although I was cataloging and making mental bookmarks, I felt discontentment and a strange feeling of sadness. I had never once been introduced to these esteemed organizations – not through school or even at home. I had no point of reference even to begin to have access to these spaces.

If I wanted to get an internship to begin my career, how would I do it? Who would I need to talk to? I couldn't think of anyone from my school, my church or even my town who had ever been to the National Democratic Convention.

While having these thoughts, I began to realize that the other students seemed more at-home than I did. They seemed to at least be familiar with these organizations, and they had enough information to be able to communicate and inquire about opportunities for their future.

But instead of letting these thoughts contribute to a feeling of inferiority, I decided then and there that I could change my destiny if I were willing to work hard and develop a passion for my future.

As I sat across the table with Congressman Thompson, I felt more than ever that it was entirely possible for me to be an African American from the State of Mississippi and go on to achieve great things in government.

My Journey to Service

I felt that I was on the precipice of something big and exciting. I credit this experience as another piece of my awakening moment.

Congressman Thompson went around the table asking each of the students about our future plans. With each narrative, my own goals swelled in size and scope.

My confidence grew so much that by the time the Congressman made it to me, I decided to grab life by the horns and use this golden opportunity to make a lasting, first impression.

I introduced myself: "My name is Duvalier Malone, and I'm from Fayette, Mississippi. I attend Jefferson County High School, and upon the acquisition of my high school diploma, I would like to attend a university in my home state and major in political science in the hopes of one day becoming a community leader in my hometown."

Congressman Thompson sat there, almost as if he were mulling over my career choice. Then he asked me, "Do you know some of the community leaders within your community? Leaders like Charles Evers?"

I answered, "Of course! I know Mr Evers."

Congressman Thompson replied by saying that Mr Evers is a great leader and the first African American mayor of my hometown of Fayette, Mississippi and had paved the way for people like himself.

When I think back about these experiences that were the birthing of my present career in public service, there are different things that stick out. One reason why this journey to Washington, DC was so important to me, was that it fostered new thoughts in my mind, and it enabled me to further develop my ambitions towards success. No longer would I have one-dimensional dreams. My landscapes had forever been broadened.

For a young boy from a poor community in Mississippi, this experience was priceless. I know now that the sparks for my calling and my passion were lit during this one trip.

I'm sometimes saddened because I wish that every young person would have the opportunity to have such a formative experience.

But we all have to take advantages of what lies right in front of us. This was my story that helped me to gain a passion for the underprivileged and seek to better myself and my community through years of public service. This is my story. It doesn't necessarily have to be yours.

If you come from a poverty-stricken community as I did, then you might not have the chance to experience dialogue or exposure to issues that transcend race, creed, and status.

However, you can still nurture the hunger for education and learn within yourself. When I attended that meeting in Washington, DC, most of the other students came from schools in more centralized communities in Mississippi; and therefore, they had access to a wealth of various opportunities that I never had.

My small school in Fayette couldn't afford to provide trips, seminars and internship experiences.

But I couldn't sit back in despair because of my lot in life that didn't provide opportunities for me. No, I had to go on the path of discovery to further educate myself and expose myself to various things that were not readily available in my community.

You have to do this too.

◆ ◆ ◆

Once I went on this path of discovery, it helped me to realize my purpose: that it was my duty to ensure that these kinds of trips and experiences would be made available for students just like me.

My experience with the essay contest and my subsequent journeys gave feature to my dreams. Now I was able to set goals that I wanted to aspire to. Of course, working as a leader in my community was out front and center.

Being able to spend time in the Nation's Capital and see for myself the change that black leadership could bring inspired me, and it helped to transform what had started as an interest into a compelling calling.

I was called by a higher power to do this work.

Chapter 2

Rural Reach

This part of the story chronicles my early adulthood, and how I began to use my platform to galvanize the community, inspiring them to seek a seat at the table, and hold their elected officials responsible for the state of the community.

Mississippi is a special place to me. It's filled with the rich and luscious countryside, and long winding and peaceful roads. The scenery is beautiful.

I can't think of a better place that would have given me the opportunity to start my adult life the right way. After I graduated from Jefferson County High School, I enrolled at Alcorn State University.

As a freshman, I went through the same experience that many others have had, coming from a small town where everyone knew each other, to a sprawling university campus with students from all over the world, and from all walks of life.

Even though Alcorn is a historically black university, we had students from Russia and other countries who had made their way to this great state to further their education.

I'm sure that this experience, interacting with so many different types of personalities, was essential to my growth as a community leader. After all, if I was expecting to represent large communities of citizens, then it was only right that I am thrust into meeting and learning to communicate effectively with various types of people.

I loved every part of it. On campus, I was focused on my studies, but I was also focused on forging connections that I knew I would carry with me for the rest of my life.

You see, it's all about reaching out and embracing others and their stories. I knew that every person that was placed in my path as a friend was there for a reason. As a person of faith, I don't believe in coincidences.

I believe that there are people who are placed in our lives for seasons, but every person that we connect with has played an integral role in helping to develop us into who we are today. I wouldn't trade those experiences for the world.

My years in college went by without incident. As focused as I was, I felt that I didn't have time to squander. I needed to make each second count because this would be a stepping stone to get me to where I knew I needed to be.

After I graduated from Alcorn with my degree in political science and pre-law, I went to Jackson State University to obtain my Masters in political science.

Yet, I still had to figure out exactly how politics would play a role in my life, but I knew that it would be essential enough that I would need a thorough understanding of this field. So I studied hard. I spent so many long nights and early mornings preparing for exams, and then finals.

And on the day I graduated from JSU, all those years of study finally paid off.

After I graduated college, I embarked on my mission to start my career in public service. I feel that I was divinely led to my career in government as a public servant where I continue to work to this very day.

Being in my government role has allowed me to develop further and hone my skills so that I can be able to give back to those in need. After all, this is what being a public servant is about.

I feel that being a public servant expanded my horizons, and opened my mind. The culture of the government has been a great home to me, and I credit this experience with helping me to form my purpose better so that I can attune myself as needed to reach the goals that I have set.

As a young person, this is important. We all will set goals for ourselves in the beginning, whether small or large. Sometimes, we may set too large a goal for ourselves, and then it seems too daunting a task to achieve.

This is why it's important to set milestones. You must sit down and plan, and decide what you want to do. Once you do that, the hard part is out of the way. You've decided on what you want to accomplish. Now all you have to do is plan it out.

The plan is just a general outline. There will be many things that will come up in your life that couldn't be predicted. These events will alter your course, and obstacles will appear and sometimes, you may have to take a slight detour.

But never forget the main objective. If an obstacle forms before you, then this is where you must use your mind to think up a solution and figure your way out of your predicament. It's not impossible. There are many people that we see in public life, who didn't get an easy ride to where they are today. They worked hard to get there, and now they can enjoy the fruits of their labor, and share those fruits with others.

In my opinion, that's where our power lies. If we truly want to dedicate our lives to the service of others, then that will drive us to continue, no matter what comes up. We will still fight to get to the finish line so that we can do what we feel we have been called to do: Which is, use our lives to improve the lives of others.

I feel confident that I reached my milestones. When I was 16, I planned to start the Dream 2 Succeed Foundation; and I did. In 2012, my foundation hosted the Southwest Mississippi Youth and Legends Ball.

My plan for the Youth and Legends Ball was to bring together accomplished community leaders who had made an impact, and impressionable young intellectuals who dreamed of becoming something more. This night would bring together these two groups of people for an evening of class, refinement and meaningful discourse.

I wanted to give the youth the same opportunities that had been given to me, and more. When I was young, and I made up my mind what I wanted to do, I had often wished that I could have had a relationship with community leaders who were already established. I wanted to benefit from their knowledge and experiences, and get advice on where this path might take me.

That's what made the Youth and Legends Ball so significant. I was giving these moments that I had wished for, to others. I truly feel that this was a powerful way to give back. This unique event would combine opportunities for underprivileged youth to practice their etiquette when in a dinner setting, and also have the opportunity to engage with some of their mentors, idols, and heroes in an unpretentious and nurturing environment.

This safe space would create a network of aspiring leaders, and their forerunners, and place a plethora of knowledge in one room where they could access it all night.

The Ball would also bring political leaders from across the state to Southwest Mississippi to further encourage, inspire and offer life-changing advice to poverty-stricken youth.

The reason I was so focused on this, was because I knew that there were many in my community who would not have the same opportunity as I had, to go and visit their state lawmakers and visit Washington, DC. They wouldn't have access to what I had access.

So my goal was to figure out a way to leverage my connections and bring those connections to the community since they were unable to get out and travel themselves. And it worked.

Congressman Greg Harper was the featured keynote speaker of the 2012 Southwest Mississippi Youth and Legends Ball. When he took the stage, he talked about our friendship and how we had known one another for years; and how in that time, he had watched me transform from an eager young thinker into a budding political maverick.

He also spoke to the students about delayed gratification and how important it is to always place God first.

As he spoke, I watched the faces in the audience as they were overcome with emotion, being able to hear what they needed to hear from someone who was an esteemed member of Mississippi's political society.

I was overcome with joy myself because this was really happening. I had dreamed of this so many years before, and here I was, living my dream, providing positivity and change for my community.

This is why I'm telling everyone who reads this book to never give up on your dream. The road will be long, and it will be hard. There will be many days when you want to lay down and just let it all go.

And as tempting as it may be to give up on the fight, you just can't let yourself do it. You must keep on, never giving up on the promises that you made to yourself.

I promised myself when I was 16 that I would improve my own life so that I could work to improve my community. There were many days when I felt as if it would be easier just to stop, and let someone else fight this fight.

But if not me, then who? There were moments when I had to tell myself how important it was that I am a representative of my community. I feel that coming from the very bottom of Jefferson County, Mississippi made me understand with crystal clarity the problems that ailed my community.

My unique experiences prepared me for community service. And so again, I asked myself on various occasions: If not me, then who?

Who would be able to adequately represent the community's needs and provide opportunities for the youth to prosper and succeed if I decided to sit back and do nothing?

Yes, it's easy to say that someone else would have stood up and worked to create these same opportunities. Maybe they would have. But by that same token, maybe they wouldn't have.

This is why it was important for me to stay in the fight. This is why it's important that you stay in the same fight. Remember, you aren't doing this for you. You're doing this to help your community.

When you have your weak moments of doubt, then this is where you should look within yourself and imagine the faces and voices of those who you love in your community, that you know depend on you to reach out and help them succeed. Let that drive you onward to your goals.

So I continued to work hard. As I worked as a community leader on one front, I worked as a social leader on another front as I endeavored tirelessly to contribute to our country as a public servant. After a few years, my hard work paid off. I was promoted and given a transfer to Washington, DC.

I was elated. I felt that my life was coming full-circle. Here I was, a young man from Mississippi, headed back to the city that helped to instill new purpose into my life.

But while I was excited about this move, I was also conflicted. I wanted and needed to take this opportunity because I knew that it would give me access to open doors that I would need in the future to be able to help my community.

Even though I realized this, I still felt like I was abandoning my family and my community in Mississippi. I knew how others might perceive this. I had been an outspoken advocate for Mississippi youth. How would I continue to do this from Washington, DC?

I had spent years giving back to the youth in my home-state, but it wasn't enough. I was helping others, but I knew that I needed a larger platform to be able to give others the opportunities that I knew they needed.

I was still considered a "small fish" in my small community in my state. To bring the right kind of positive influence that would be needed to change my community, I would have to go and establish relationships with other influencer's that would be willing to aid me in this cause.

As I came to these realizations, it helped to quiet the discomfort in my mind. I knew that if I could not help myself, then I had no hope ever to help others.

So I made a move. I packed up my belongings, and I gave an emotional farewell to my home state. Perhaps "farewell" is the wrong word to use. I always planned to return; and upon my return, I plan to have resources at my disposal to be able to elevate my community and other communities.

After moving to Washington DC and getting settled, I began to reflect. There had to be a way that I could live in this great city, but still reach back home to my community and provide help and inspiration.

So what did I want? I wanted to create a change in my community. I knew that for that change to happen, I would need to get involved with providing education to the people.

It's like the great Nelson Mandela once said: "Education is the most powerful weapon that we can use to change the world."

Change the world. Those words echoed in my mind again and again. This would be a feat of incredible magnitude, but I believe that every one of us has our part to play in the fight to change our world for the better.

You that are reading this: You have a part in this change. Sometimes, to find out where your path leads, you have to look in the most peculiar of places. You have to look inside of yourself.

That's what I began to do. I began to search internally within myself to find where my path would lead. If education was needed to create positive change within my community, then I needed to figure out a way to provide that.

I wanted to make myself an instrument of this great change. I had been on radio and television before while working with my foundation to create opportunities for poverty-stricken youth. So I knew the awesome power of media.

I could go into a room at any given time and speak, and I would only be able to communicate with as many people as the room could hold. But if I went on the radio and spoke, I could speak to hundreds and thousands of people.

I knew then what I needed to do. I decided to start a brand new radio show, which would be titled "Rural Reach". The title was a very apt description of what I wanted to do. I wanted to reach the people in rural communities back home, and provide information that was not readily available or accessible in these communities.

I also had intentions of starting a conversation that would help students to understand the process through which policy was formed in Washington. After all, the policy that was formed in the great halls of Congress would be what would provide a future shaping of these rural communities. So I felt that it was important for everyone to gain an understanding of this process.

This was new for me. I had never imagined that I would serve in an educational capacity. But that's how things sometimes work. We place goals in our lives, and to reach those goals, many times we wind up having to do things that we never saw ourselves doing.

I knew that to be a community leader, that meant that I would have to provide the education and information to those people that I was trying to help.

To break the vicious cycle of ignorance in such a small community, I would need to try to break the stronghold of corruption that placed limits on the hopes and dreams of the people.

So I decided that this would be another focus of the "Rural Reach" radio show: To shine a light on the corruption that existed in my hometown and empower others by showing them the might within media.

I've always believed that if you're willing to stand up and fight for what is right, then your voice will become the beacon of hope for others. If you make a stand, rest assured: There will be others who will stand with you.

I just needed my community to understand the power in this, and to realize the importance of becoming engaged in their future.

As I began to look for guests for "Rural Reach," I reached out to my friend, Congressman Harper. Not only was he a part of the Southwest Mississippi Youth and Legends Ball, but he also agreed to be the very first guest on my radio show.

On the show, Congressman Harper talked about the various ways to improve education, decrease the unemployment rate, further stimulate economic development in Southwest Mississippi, and he also shared his views on reducing spending in America.

His views were fascinating and enthralling to the audience.

Over the course of my career as a community leader, people have always wanted to know how I was able to create and sustain relationships with such decorated politicians – in particular, my relationship with Congressman Harper.

My reply to them was that, I first met Congressman Harper when I was in college, in the very infancy of my professional career. I never angled or calculated to make friends in high places. The friendships that I have with my mentors, no matter how accomplished they are, is one that is rooted in scholarship, public service and a love for policy.

Here I was, working to make a difference in my community. I spoke out and made the necessary noise for change. In each of our lives, there will come a time when you must decide if you will idly stand by or if you will stand up and speak out and let your voice be heard.

Idly standing by means that you are contributing to the problem. If you are blessed with sight to see what ails your community, and you do nothing, you are complicit.

If you can see the issues that lie before you, then you owe it to yourself, and you owe it to your community to stand up and be heard. Make your voice as loud as it needs to be in order to get the attention of those who you are trying to reach.

This is what the great leaders of our past did. Dr Martin Luther King, Jr. stood up, and he let his voice be heard, even though it was dangerous. Even though there was a possibility that he could lose his life, he refused to let himself be silenced by fear. He refused to be silenced by those who he knew were wrong.

If we want to prove that we truly do give a damn about our communities, then we have to be as courageous as Dr King. No matter the risk, we can't remain silent. If we don't fight for change, then who will?

These are the kinds of messages that I wanted to impart to my community as I spoke through the radio. And I refused to stop there. I took advantage of whatever medium was placed before me.

When the medium was newspaper media, I wrote columns to reach the people. I held town hall forums to encourage the community to come out and discuss the issues and get involved.

As I did this, I pondered over more ways that I could use my voice and platform to help drive change in my home state. I didn't know it yet, but a major change loomed before me in the coming months.

Many times when you work as a community leader, you don't think of the work that you do regarding receiving awards and honors. You do this work because you care deeply about your community.

So when I was selected to receive the Top 50 under 40 Award from the Mississippi Business Journal, it caught me off guard. Not in a negative way, because this was a great honor. But I wasn't in the mind-frame of even thinking about accepting awards for the type of work that I do.

I believe that to be a leader in one's community; you have to go into it with the realization that this is a labor of love. It's the type of labor that will endear the community to you, but first, you must endear yourself to that community, putting their needs above yours.

But when you form that type of attachment to the people that you represent, you will find that they will look for ways to show their appreciation for you. They will want to show you that they support you as you support them.

This award came when I didn't have anything like this on my mind. I was actually in deep thought, contemplating the changes that I would need to make to become more effective for my community. I was internally evaluating my growth, strengths, and weaknesses.

It's always important that you self-reflect. You must be willing to face the mirror and look at yourself to figure out what you can do to help yourself; because if you don't help yourself, you can't help your community.

Here's what I found when I did my self-reflection. Keep in mind that this was a few years after my move to Washington, DC. I was now 29 years old, and I came to the realization that even though I had been spending my time supporting my community, and trying to reach back to my community, that I had played it safe up until this point.

What I mean by this is: I hadn't tackled any controversial issues. The issues of poverty and education are nominally embraced by all. No one is going to attack and criticize you if you tell them that your dream is to provide education for your community and to empower your community financially.

But even though fighting for these issues had made me a credible leader in the deep south, I still felt that there was more that I should be doing.

It wasn't that I was avoiding controversial issues. I just prioritized what I felt mattered most to my community. That's what I spent my time speaking out on.

It was just that now, I started to realize that I must lend my voice to other critical issues that affect my community. So in April 2016, I traveled home to Mississippi to receive the Top 50 under 40 award.

It was by happenstance that upon my arrival, I learned of a great injustice that the Governor and other lawmakers had done.

Mississippi's political leaders had decided to pass a law called HB 1523. This law would give businesses the authority to decide not to serve members of the LGBTQ community.

I was shocked and horrified – and saddened. I had spent years tackling the issues of poverty and education, and never once had I even thought to tackle an issue that was close to me personally.

I am a gay man from Mississippi. This was never a secret. I never tried to hide it. But I will admit that I never embraced it publicly. Never before had it been an issue, but at this point, I came to the stark realization that I had made a mistake.

Because of my silence, my community was unaware of the HB 1523 law. As I walked down the sidewalks of my hometown, I realized that they were disconnected from this issue. They didn't know, and they didn't realize the effect that this law would have on the lives of young men and women, and the effect that it would have on businesses in our state.

Just from the perspective of public relations, this would be a bad move for Mississippi; not to mention, the fact that this would be taking a step backward in civil rights.

To refuse to serve someone because of their sexual orientation is wrong. And this is where I started to think seriously about what I was willing to use my platform for.

Up to this point, this issue would be the most controversial issue that I had ever used my status as a community leader to speak on. I felt that if I were to make this move, I would be jumping right out of the nest and spreading my wings to find out whether or not I could fly finally.

This wasn't an issue that I could take a lukewarm stance on. No, my position here would have to be strong, loud and steadfast. That was the only thing that could provide the type of push back that would be needed to fight this bill.

So as I made up my mind to do this, I realize now that this was the moment where I finally started to not give a damn about what people think about me. I knew people would whisper and they would talk. But I no longer cared.

I realized that to be the type of leader for my community that I had dreamed about a long time ago, it meant that I would have to take stances that were controversial and that might even be unpopular. But that's what this job is about.

There will be many times when you have to struggle within yourself to figure out what you want to be known for. I wanted to be known for standing up in the struggle for those who didn't have a voice. They didn't have an outlet to express themselves to the world. But I did.

And I wanted to use my outlet to be the mouthpiece for these individuals who had been silenced. Through me, they would be silenced no longer.

I had to come to grips with where I would stand, and you will face situations where you must do the same. Make the right decision. I know you're probably wondering, which decision is the right one? But trust me: When you see it, you will know. You'll know what you need to do to be the voice of everyone in your community.

So I drafted a letter to Mississippi to speak out against this bill. I knew that the only way I would be taken seriously was if I lived my truth. I knew that I had to come out to the world about my sexual orientation, and about the man that I love.

I was counseled against this. My media counsel asked me, "Are you sure? Do you know that this could affect your ability to run for a political office in the future?"

I acknowledged that what she said was true, but I couldn't stay silent because of fear. I refused to stand idly by while a young child in Mississippi commits suicide because of a lack of representation because they aren't able to see themselves as being deserving of love.

So I decided I would do my part in this fight. I wrote a powerful column where I spoke of my love for Mississippi. But I denounced these hateful acts that were emanating from our state legislators.

I spoke proudly of my soul mate, Adrian. I talked about my pride in being a gay man from Mississippi, and how I am a product of everything that this state has to offer.

I didn't shy away from admitting my shortcomings. I knew that I had failed many. By not taking a stance on LGBTQ issues, it made me complicit. I was a silent accomplice to the atmosphere in our state, which made many think that it was okay to discriminate against individuals because of their sexual orientation.

Whenever these issues were mentioned in my presence, I simply said nothing. I realize now that I was wrong. It was wrong for me to watch as many of my peers suffered, while I sat in a position to help, and didn't.

So I was more than willing to accept my failures and do what was necessary to redeem myself by fighting for this cause the best way I knew how. I would continue to use my voice and my platform to call out the governor and his political minions who turned their backs on the very people that they are sworn to represent.

If love and tolerance were to be ejected from the halls of the State Congress, then no one was safe. Today, it's the LGBTQ community. Who would it be tomorrow?

So you see, I made a mistake, and I was more than willing to declare my shortcomings publicly. This is something that all community leaders must be willing to do.

We are human, and we will make mistakes. But how will we handle that situation? Will we stubbornly refuse to acknowledge our wrong, or will we come out and condemn our actions as we condemn the actions of others who seek to eradicate the love and tolerance that binds our communities together?

I chose to come out and be transparent. I sought forgiveness for my mistakes, and I pledged myself to this cause forever, that I would do my part to combat intolerance and hate.

When you make a mistake, you must do the same. You must be willing to protect the integrity of your mission by acknowledging when you are wrong. By doing this, you protect your community, and it adds to the depth of your character as an activist and community leader.

These experiences will make you stronger. These experiences will force you to grow, and they will forge you into what your community needs you to be.

Chapter 3

Our Seat at the Table

I use my platform to galvanize the community, inspiring them to seek a seat at the table, and hold their elected officials responsible for the state of the community. But I realize that I am not immune to the same criticisms. I understand that I too have been given a platform, and I am equally as responsible for using my platform to create the change that I have championed.

As I looked for new ways to create opportunities for my community, I pondered more about what the platform of a social activist and community leader was even for. As I recovered from my misstep regarding gay rights, which I considered to be a black eye on my social justice record, I decided to focus myself on the various issues that affect those who I represent.

I had to learn to forgive myself, and it took time. But as you go through life, you will make mistakes. I decided to use this learning tool to better myself and improve upon my skills to be a better community leader and activist.

I would tell anyone that being a community leader is a learning experience. You are going to get to the point where you sometimes need to get back the basics and remember that before all of the awards and ceremonies; it was just you and the people.

The people are what matter. Not you, and not me. The people are why we do what we do. When I first started this journey, it was because I didn't want anyone to have to suffer the way that I did.

I watched helplessly as poverty wreaked havoc on my family throughout the first part of my life. Growing up, I wished that someone would have been there to alleviate what drove deep division between my mother and father.

But no one was there for my family. So that's why I have committed myself to being there for other families.

I want people to feel that they can call on me if necessary. If they are facing roadblocks in their lives and they see no way around them, I want to be an instrument to help.

This is who we are when we take on the mantle of community leaders. We are guardians that serve as watchmen to do our best to ensure that the people who we represent are cared for and provided for.

See, I know from experience that the only thing that separates a poverty-stricken community from a middle-class community is chance and circumstance. I strongly believe that if these low-income communities were given the same hand up as everyone else, then they would thrive and be successful too.

That's the only barrier: Our circumstances. Everyone must realize that these families that are in these communities are gifted. There are some of the most intelligent children you will ever meet that are growing up in impoverished communities.

They just haven't been given the same opportunities as everyone else.

But that's where community leaders and activists come in. We go to the people to find out what is needed, and then we use our circle of influence to find out how we can bring resources to the community.

So I went to the people to pick their brains and find out what they needed the most.

Politicians feel that they know better than everyone else. They feel that they know what the people need, more than the people know themselves. But I refuse to get caught in that cycle of self-importance.

That's the reason why many poverty-stricken communities are stagnant now. We have elected political leaders who have lost touch with the very people who put them where they are today. We gave opportunities to many who simply forgot about us once they were elected into office.

That's always the danger of being a public figure. It's incredibly easy to get caught up in your hype. When you see yourself on television or see your name in the papers, it's easy to begin to think that this is about you first, and the people second.

Politicians aren't the only ones who fall into this trap. Community leaders and activists are also prone to making the same mistakes. This is why we have to be extra careful, and remain focused and grounded at all times.

One of the ways that I have been able to stay grounded was through my mother and making sure that I was never completely disconnected from my past.

Even though I often talk about my personal history and the tragedy of my youth, I see that there are a lot of people who think that I have regrets.

I don't. I can't wish away anything that happened in my past, and I would never want to. All of those experiences contributed to who I am today. If I had grown up in a middle-class neighborhood and went to the best schools in the state, then I probably would never have gotten involved with social activism.

Sometimes it's hard to empathize with a life that you've never led. I'm not saying that it's impossible, only that it can be difficult. But when you come from the life that you talk about, and when you can form a genuine connection with the people, then you are qualified to represent them in political and social circles.

In my situation, it was easy for me to decide that I would stand up and get involved. I always knew that I was destined to reach back to give others the opportunities that I never had. I wanted to help other young people so that they wouldn't have to experience what I experienced.

So as I tried to focus on the issues that mattered to the people, I began to notice the common thread that existed among small Mississippi towns and cities: Poverty.

I remember reading in college classes about the problem that many people in my home state were left to deal with. Mississippians don't have access to a wide range of jobs, and our economy is lacking.

But what I could not understand was how these same issues that affected us 40 and 50 years ago are still here, with no progress made at all. The average family in Jefferson County, Mississippi in 2018 is at the same place financially as a family in the same location in 1998.

That's twenty years of either little progress or no progress at all. So as I examined this closely, I began to wonder: What the hell are our political leaders doing?

We have some in our state legislature that has been there for 20 and 30 years. What have they accomplished to improve the lives of their constituents?

There was a time when I would be more tactful and careful while addressing this topic; but as I see the conditions of my community spiraling further downward, I realize that we don't have time for tact and carefulness. Not right now.

There are very real issues, and troubles that affect the lives of these poor communities, and the representation that we have received so far from our political leadership is simply insufficient. We are not receiving what we need to be able to capitalize on an investment into the improvement of our communities.

It's easy to blame our political leaders, but the truth is that it's not all their fault. We gave license to this behavior when we willingly gave up our seats at the table. We enabled our political leaders to feel that they didn't have to tackle this issue.

We fell in love with apathy, and we didn't care what happened in our state's political chambers as long as we couldn't see it affecting us. But what we didn't understand was that it doesn't matter whether or not you can see it. It may not even affect you right now at this moment; but at some point, what happens in our state's political offices will trickle down, and it will affect us either positively or negatively.

I have often tried to get others to grasp the importance of this. That's why I continue to use the phrase "seat at the table." It's important. The people's political leverage is one of the most important things that we have.

But what happens when we don't use it, or even worse, are afraid to use it?

I believe that this is what has contributed to the conditions of poverty-stricken communities all across our state. Unfortunately, in some cases, political leaders will do what they can get away with unless they are held accountable by the people.

If the public refuses to turn a watchful eye to the happenings of our political offices, then we are going against the American idea of society. We can't just go vote every election and expect everything to work out on its own magically.

That's not how this works. We have to get involved, and we have to stay involved at all times. We have to encourage our young people to get involved in political affairs at a young age, even before they can vote. If they get involved with it now, then they will have enough experience to know how to leverage their power as an American citizen to improve their lives in the future.

This is the work of a community leader and activist. This is where you come in, and you serve as the connection between the community and their interests. There are going to be some who fight you. Sometimes you will have to metaphorically drag a politician kicking and screaming before the people, to make them pay attention to their constituents.

I have no problem doing this. I often tell people that I will be upfront and honest at all times. I understand politics, and I know that many times you have to come to common grounds on particular issues. But when the lives of the people in my community are at stake, then I have no time for political gamesmanship.

We know that we are in dire need of change. The people that are in political positions have the power to affect change if they are brave enough to step out on faith and take a chance.

I learned early on the power and strength of faith. I had my mother as an example, to show me that if you just believe and trust God, then He will take care of you. Our politicians must trust and believe too. If you do this, then I know that God will help you take care of His people.

You see, much of what we do is divinely led. I truly believe this. I feel deep within myself that when we are working on behalf of the people to try to better their lives, then we are working towards a divine goal.

So I have chosen to inspire my community and other communities to get involved again. We can't sit out when it comes to our future. We have to get involved, and we have to be willing to work for the change that we all say we want.

There's a lot of dialogue that we must have. We have to be willing to sit at the table and listen to viewpoints that are different from what we believe. And they must be willing to listen to us. This is called exchanging views. This is how goals are met within our governmental system of checks and balances.

Yes, there will be debates and ideological differences, but that's what makes America who we are. That's the very fiber that holds us together: The ability to come together and have different views, but still be willing to work towards a unified objective of bettering ourselves and our communities.

We have to be willing to look at our political leaders with an objective eye. And politicians don't have the right to be angry if the people who put them in office decide that they want to examine their investment.

Political leaders represent you. They are not in political office to represent themselves. They are there to represent the interests of the people. And the people have the right to ensure that politicians are serving their best interests.

I won't stop encouraging citizens to demand a seat at the table. I won't. And political leaders can't deny the people their rightful seat.

There are laws in place that have been there since the beginning of this country, that give citizens the right to representation. We have the right to demand that the political leaders represent us the way that we want them to.

If they refuse, then we have mechanisms in place if we receive no cooperation. We can vote them out of office.

This is why it's important that community leaders do their best to ensure a high turnout for elections. If political leaders know that the community is watching them closely and that they are planning to get involved in the political process in record-breaking numbers, then I guarantee you that they will be very careful with their actions.

They won't want to do anything that could jeopardize their political futures. This is the type of leverage that we must teach the people that they have.

There's a huge educational component that must be realized here. The people have lost their power. But here's the thing: The power is still there. It's just that the people don't know that they can access their power.

We go through highs and lows in history, and I'm sad to say that we are currently experiencing a low. What we are seeing is complacency. During the Civil Rights movement, there was a concerted and visible effort to disenfranchise American citizens. Today, that same effort is afoot; but it's less visible. It's hidden now. And because the people don't see an outright manifestation of the efforts to strip their rights, they don't see a reason to get involved in this fight.

Our community has come a long way, but we lost something during this journey. We lost our passion and our concern for our civic future.

Now everyone is concentrating on the rat-race, which is completely understandable. Everyone has bills to pay, and their immediate worry is putting food on the table - not worrying about the actions of someone in the State or Nation's Capital.

I understand because it was the same with my family. When I was growing up, we couldn't worry ourselves about the actions of the governor. We were too busy trying to figure out where the next meal would come from.

So that's why I go to such lengths to stress the importance of solving the issues of poverty. Once a family no longer has to worry about their own survival, then they can concentrate on the better parts of life, such as the elections and their education and their health.

But as long as they are suffering and searching for ways out of the hole that they were born into, then it's almost impossible to expect them to strive for more. They are already doing all they can to not slip into the abyss.

This is the reason I do what I do. It's because I've been there, and I know the stresses that come along with being in poverty. So I feel that it's my duty to educate my peers and encourage you all to look and search for the solution.

It's not going to be easy. As the old saying goes, if it were easy, everyone would be doing it. I strongly feel that if the solution to poverty were something simple and as easy as 1, 2, 3, then it would have been done a long time ago.

But just because it hasn't happened yet, doesn't make it impossible. No, it just means that we have to work harder to come up with a solution to the problems that exist.

I know that we can do it. We have access to too many things. We have the Internet at our fingertips. Research is easier now than it has ever been. We all must be willing to tackle these issues together.

It's a problem, but the answer is probably right in front of us, and we just don't see it. But one thing I do know is that the solution will require our political leaders to get involved and lead us to a better place.

I remember traveling to the Mississippi Delta to film the documentary "Clarksdale at the Crossroad." As I drove through this poor community, it literally hurt me to my heart that people were still living this way.

I sometimes wonder: Has Governor Bryant ever driven through these streets? Has he or any of our elected politicians ever seen with their own eyes, the conditions that exist in so many communities across our state? And if they have seen it, then why aren't they doing anything to solve this crisis?

There should be task-force after task-force assigned with one objective: That objective should be, nothing but solving the problem of poverty in this state.

This isn't anything that I haven't said before. I addressed this in column after column, using my voice and my platform unapologetically to bring attention to this crisis.

I spoke again and again about the fact that Mississippi has the highest poverty rate in the entire country. I spoke on how over 200,000 children in Mississippi live below the national poverty line.

These numbers should be enough to spur our leaders into action, to try to fix whatever is broken in this state. But instead, they choose to turn a blind eye to the plight of the people.

I don't like to say that they don't care, but I honestly feel that they are saying it to me. Actions speak louder than words.

How can anyone run for office and not make poverty the main linchpin of their political platform? Poverty should be a mainstay in every political campaign across the nation until it no longer exists.

We should go to sleep thinking of solutions, and we should wake up with it on our mind. During our workdays, we should still be thinking of ways to improve the lives of ourselves and our neighbors.

So many of us want to bring justice to our legal system, others want to eliminate racism, and others are trying to improve our schools, but let's synchronize our concepts of hope.

These are all very noble issues to fight for. I'm fighting for these issues too. But I never forget that the central topic is the fact that all of these people are poor. They are disenfranchised, and they are suffering every day.

That's why all of us need to work together. We need to put our minds together and look at this problem from every angle to find an adequate solution.

And this isn't just an issue that must be tackled by community leaders and social activists. No, all leaders in every facet of life must be encouraged to join this movement.

I'm asking all of our leaders to get involved in this, at every level. If you're a coach, guess what? You're in a position of leadership for those young men and women who look to you for guidance.

If you're a mentor, get involved. Look at those that you've committed yourself to mentoring, and realize that they look to you for leadership and advice for the path that they are traveling in their lives.

Even if you're just a role model, you are a person that has the trust and the ear of other people, who will be willing to listen to you and your viewpoint.

Your influence extends far beyond what you think. You have so much more influence than you realize.

But how are you using it?

Imagine if we all used our influence to create change. There would be no limit to what we can achieve.

We should all use our platforms to initiate change in our communities on these pressing issues. Our communities need our help to move forward.

There is no need to fight each other. I see so many people in the community that are content with simply sitting back and criticizing others, instead of putting in the work to make a difference.

No one is above criticism. Please understand that. We all can use criticism at different points to make ourselves better and to improve our platform, and keep our swords sharp. I truly believe that this will enable us to be better aids to the community. If we are constantly pushed to improve our program and make ourselves great, then that greatness will extend to the larger community.

But what I don't appreciate is those who immaturely criticize a person and a platform because of personal dislike. There's no room for that in what we are trying to do.

I keep driving home the point that this isn't about any one person. This is about our community. The community doesn't have time for our bickering and constant back and forth about the things that don't even matter.

It wastes time, and it takes away from the work that we should all be focused on.

We don't even have time to be divided on our belief systems. Some of us are Christians, some of us are Jewish, some of us are Muslims. What does that have to do with us working together to improve our community?

We can't let ourselves stay divided into our various ideologies and differences; because no matter your belief, I know that you believe that all human beings deserve to have the best life that they can have. That's the central component of every religion that I've ever run across: to improve the lives of the people.

Well then, since we all have this common thread and it runs through religious circles as well as social circles, I'm asking us all to grab hold to that thread and let's work together to fix the brokenness that exists in the lives of so many.

Let's put our differences aside and work towards that common goal and I promise you that we will start to see that we have more in common than we think. We are all God's children, and we all should be focused on extending the blessing that God has given us to others.

At this point, you might be thinking that I have a calling. I do, but it's not a religious calling. It's a calling to this life of community service. I'm not a preacher. I'm a believer, and I will do everything I can to help others to believe in the power of themselves, and in the hope that life can be better.

This is why I'm so hard on our political leaders, but it's not personal. It's just that I know what individuals in poverty communities are experiencing every day of their lives, and just as something was awakened inside of me, I now seek to awaken others.

Elected officials should not play politics with us. It's almost criminal to see how some of their constituents live, and then see political leaders that don't care.

I ask this question: How can your political leaders sleep at night? They shouldn't be able to. I have many sleepless nights because of my singular devotion to improving the lives of the people who I represent. There are many times when this is all I can think about, and I can't get work done because I'm wrestling with these thoughts of how to better my community.

I understand that it's a balancing act, and sometimes our political leaders are more loyal to the political action committees (PACs) that helped them secure the office that they now hold. But if those financial backers of their campaign are not interested in helping them to empower the people, then what is their real goal?

I'm suspicious of anyone that wants to secure political favor for their own personal gain, and they have no interest in tending to the needs of the masses. I'm left wondering, what is the goal of these political leaders?

Politicians should break the bonds that bind them to parties that have no ties to the community. Instead, they should refocus themselves on their constituents and work hard to eradicate poverty, create jobs and improve our schools. If they do this, the people will reward politicians over and over for their sincere dedication to tackling the issues that they face.

We hope that our political leaders will do the right thing.

To my fellow community leaders and social activists: We hope that our politicians will involve themselves in the lives of everyday citizens, and do their best to improve what they see, but we can't wait on them.

In the spirit of Dr King, we must be willing to apply pressure to force our political leaders to consider what we have to say, and give the people their seat at the table. This is why I spoke earlier on the importance of mobilizing and getting out the vote.

My generation especially seems not entirely to grasp just how powerful their vote is. This is why I want to challenge our educators, pastors, and community leaders to start using your voice to influence others and educate them on just how much a difference they can make with their vote.

There's a precedent that's been set for using the voting population to force political leaders to meet at the table with them. When Dr King was able to amass and galvanize a large number of citizens to become involved in the cause for civil rights, he got the attention of President John F. Kennedy. President Kennedy, just like any other political leader, had to take note when he saw the numbers that were behind this movement.

Well, we must do the same today. If we can show our political leaders that we have the numbers behind our cause, then that forces them to meet with us and listen. We simply have to get their attention.

This means sounding a rallying cry in your community to let the people know that now is the time to get involved. You have to rekindle their interest in their civic duty. Yes, many people are going through a lot, but you as a community leader have to figure out how to influence them to want to be involved in a social cause.

You will have to talk to them and communicate clearly what your intentions are, and why they should support you. You have to break through their barrier and make them understand that this is necessary to their well-being.

Like I said before, there's definitely an educational component. Sometimes you will have to teach them the process and show plainly how their involvement can tip the scale in their favor. You have to show them how their presence and the presence of their family and friends and neighbors at a political event is a show of power. When large groups of people show up, those in political offices have no choice but to take note.

So you have to convince them of this. It can be a trying effort, I know. You're trying to teach people why they should be more concerned about the political process than their immediate situation.

It's a hard sell. I know that when I was growing up, and we were in the middle of a tumultuous domestic household as well as a poverty-stricken living situation, it would have been next to impossible to convince my mother to drop what she was doing and come out to a political rally.

I'm not saying that a resourceful community activist could not have persuaded her—just that it would have been difficult. But I believe that's what we train for when we decide to take on the mantle of activism in our communities. We train to deal with every situation, no matter how difficult they may seem.

We are here to help the people by providing opportunities and using our connections to open doors. We can't force anyone to walk through the door that we open, but I do believe in using my political charisma and social aptitude to convince and persuade where I can. I don't mind convincing someone to do something that I know will help them in the long run.

And I truly feel that if I'm able to get a family to come to one of these events and see with their own eyes the power that they wield, then they will come again. It will no longer be something taboo that they read about in their history books. No, it will be something that is credible and life-changing; and you just never know. They may bring a child, and an event like this might spark the child's interests in having a political future.

So there are a lot of potential benefits that come along with a family taking an interest in the political process. I believe that this is an instance where we should pay it forward. By investing our time and energy into a family, we are creating a ripple of positive energy that will extend out to their social circle and then down the line; they may choose to do what we do.

They may choose to get involved in a life of public service. And at the end of the day, that's what we want and need. We don't necessarily even need them to get involved full-time. But if we can help the next generation to take an interest in their civic duty and to be politically conscious, then I believe that we can move to improve our communities at a faster pace.

Community leaders and social activists can do the heavy lifting. But we still need some level of involvement from everyone in the community. That's how a movement grows. There are always going to be the people at the center of the movement, and then the larger masses are there to get involved when they are needed.

But it's up to us to show a shining example of what civic duty looks like. We have to go first and do the hard part of making a stand, even when we have minimal support.

The lack of support that we receive isn't because we are wrong. I've had events where only a handful of people showed up. But that wasn't because I was making a stand on something that was bad for the community. It was simply evidence of the larger issue, which is the lack of knowledge, concern or involvement that has a grip on our communities.

So this is why I'm encouraging you to drive home the importance of every citizen becoming involved in the political process. Encourage them to seek a seat at the table. Tell them to demand it.

When our political leaders operate irresponsibly, then it's up to us to demand that they are held accountable. We want to work with them. That's how we make our communities better. But we want them to recognize that they have to do the right thing.

And if they aren't willing to do the right thing, then we have a political process that makes everyone replaceable. We want someone in office that's going to sit down at the table with us and listen to the needs of the community. The time to get started on this is now.

Let's demand our seat at the table. The change starts with us.

Chapter 4

Symbols of Hate

After much reflection, I decided to lend my voice to a dangerous movement: The fight against racism and hatred. I put much on the line by speaking boldly, challenging the governor of Mississippi to denounce the racist history of the state. I stood at the forefront of the movement to remove the Confederate symbol from the Mississippi state flag.

Charleston. It's amazing how just one word can cause you to remember such vivid and horrible imagery. It's almost like saying Hiroshima, or Aleppo. It's right there on the world stage because of one person who made a choice to change the world forever.

I haven't had the opportunity to visit Charleston yet, but by all accounts, it's a beautiful historic place, rich in culture and history.

But it's also the site of a terrible mass murder that, whether we want to admit it or not, added to the ever-expanding gulf between the right and the left.

When Dylann Roof decided to murder nine African Americans inside their church while they studied the Bible, did he know the effect that his murderous act would have on the world?

No. After all, how could he? Dylann Roof is not a well-studied or well-read young man. If he were, then I would venture to say that there is no way that he would have ever committed himself to the cause of bigotry and intolerance.

You see, those are concepts that are steeped in ignorance. To commit yourself to such vile ideas, you have to close your mind to knowledge and history. And that's why I genuinely believe that when he did what he did, Dylann Roof had no foresight. The only thing that existed to him at that moment was the people that he wanted to kill.

Being a witness to an event like that does something to you. Of course, all tragedies affect us in many ways. We don't even have to be there. Reading about it or seeing the aftermath on television can shake us to our very foundation.

When you realize that there are people that want to kill you for no other reason than the way you look, it affects you—deeply.

Probably every other African American in this country and I felt the despair that rushed through our bodies almost as quickly as those nine lives that were extinguished.

The despair leads to hopelessness; and then you have to ask yourself: How is it that in the 21st century, we can still be victims of barbaric notions such as racism?

How does this happen? Where did society go wrong?

As I watched the 24/7 round-the-clock news coverage of this tragedy, so many thoughts rushed through my mind. What did those nine people think as they felt their lives slipping away?

Maybe they wondered to themselves the same question that I asked to myself: Perhaps they were attempting to figure out, why: Why are people still fighting to extinguish the lives of their fellow Americans because of the color of their skin?

As I thought over these things, I began to feel something happen inside of me. I felt sick. I felt trapped.

I felt helpless.

All those things that I felt, I would never wish on another person. I would never want someone to feel that something needed to be done but there was nothing that they could do.

It was as if I was back in the 1960's, experiencing the Birmingham church bombing that killed four little girls, or the assassination of Medgar Evers.

I thought about the many stories that my grandmother shared with me. Many times we sat and talked, and she told me of the killings and the murders that happened. She would sometimes shake as she described the anger and the fear that so many felt.

At this moment, I finally understood; and even that shook me—the fact that long after the events of the Civil Rights movement, we still faced the fear of racism and hatred.

Then something snapped. I thought back to all of my experiences up to this point—the way I pulled myself out of poverty, how I had provided opportunities for others - and that's when I knew that I had to use my voice to combat this evil that has persisted in our society for far too long.

I needed to do my part in this fight. But what would I do?

It's disturbing how so many problems leave you wondering where to start. It's as if there's so much that's wrong, that it's almost impossible to decide on which issue takes precedence. And when you finally do make a decision, there's always the possibility that you chose the wrong problem to fight at this particular time.

There are so many things that you must consider.

Here I was, finally deciding to make a stand against racism and hatred. In the shadow of terrible acts, I struggled to shine a light that would help to lead us out of the darkness.

Being from Mississippi, I understood how racism works. The entire history of our state was built on the backs that racism bent and destroyed.

I know this state of racism, and I know what's at stake here. We struggle with finding the balance in racial harmony. Yes, we've seen a lot of progress. Mississippi has come a long way. We've made extreme leaps and bounds.

But now it seems that we are at a crossroads. We are at a defining period that will directly impact our state's future.

And here I was, trying to figure out how I factored into all of this. I had been blessed with so much, and I was still searching for the way to give all that I could give to my community and my state.

As I began to tell my friends that I was planning something, many of them voiced opposition to me – not because they felt what I wanted to do was wrong. No, it wasn't that.

It was because they were afraid for me.

You see, everyone knows that sacrifice has always been a theme of the Civil Rights movement. The sacrifice of career, endeavors, and sometimes even being willing to sacrifice your own life to ensure that the lives of others are bettered.

We've seen it many times: Dr Martin Luther King, Jr and Medgar Evers. Brave men who stood up and put their own lives on the line for a cause that was greater than them.

That concept was always incredible and yet frightening to even me. Not saying that I would place myself on the level of those two great men, but what I was about to do would be incredibly dangerous.

This danger is what my friends sensed and cautioned.

The fact of the matter is that there are those in the world who want to harm others based on their race, based on their sexual orientation, and based on their stances on various issues.

And after all, this is Mississippi. I greatly champion the fact that this state has gone through many changes and that we are better now than we have ever been. However, I would be a fool to completely disregard the dark history that still manages to permeate the thoughts and feelings of people who have extreme emotional ties to what they feel is their heritage.

I've never considered myself to be naive. I'm simply hopeful. As a person that came from the bottom of poverty, I've always been optimistic for a better way, a better solution and a better people.

But I've been proven wrong. Charleston proved me wrong. And while my modern day concept of justice would be considered mainstream in America, there are always those who exist in the fringe regions of our society that don't subscribe to those mainstream notions.

So there lies the reality that I had to come to grips. Yes, I must make this stand for what I believe is right. But while making this stand, I have to be willing to accept the danger that comes along with being a bold, public figure. I have to be willing to be scrutinized by those who hate everything that I stand for.

So was I willing to take this step? I will admit, it wasn't easy. Knowing that everything could change in the blink of an eye was somewhat unsettling. I had never faced anything like this before.

If I decided to do this, I would be a vocal, outspoken activist putting it all on the line.

I've never been a selfish person. Not at all. I've always been willing to give all of myself to my friends and my family.

But this would be different. This stand would be me giving myself to an entire state of people with differing opinions, different values, and moral yardsticks.

To step to the forefront of any movement is a huge responsibility. I would tell anyone that has aspirations of being a public servant and a community leader, that you must make sure that this is 100% what you want for your life.

There will be many distractions along the way, and you will have to make many hard decisions. The job is often thankless and perilous.

But if you know deep down within yourself that you have what it takes to step to the forefront and make noise for change, then do it. Be that beacon of justice.

Inspect yourself and determine what you have to offer the world. If you can stand for the oppressed and be a stronghold against the forces that exist to silence them, then do it.

Always remember that this is a work that is ongoing. Unfortunately, it doesn't stop; and things will happen at the most inopportune moments of your life. But you should stay prepared at all times, just in case you are called upon to help a family in need, or to vocalize the needs of your community.

Put others before yourself as you selflessly serve the under-served. There is no greater reward than pushing for change and seeing that change manifest first in policy, and then later in tangible needs that are met in your community.

And if you decide to fight against bigotry and intolerance, here's what I found to be true.

Of course, bigotry and intolerance is nothing new. It's an outdated concept, which although it has survived into our time, is condemned by anyone who holds tight to basic fundamental American values.

I don't think that I have a direct claim to this fight.

I like to think of it as a fight where we must all play our part. If we truly care about the direction of our society, then we must stand up and be seen and heard, and be willing to stand on our principles. Anything less than this is trite and insincere.

Is it dangerous? Yes, but taking a stand on anything that could advance society has always been dangerous, and sometimes change makers pay with their lives.

But when Dr Martin Luther King, Jr stood up and decided to make a stand, he did so with a sincere desire to either stand up for what he believed in or die for what he believed.

And in death, he has been immortalized.

Years after Dr King's assassination, his ideas and his views and his legacy live on regardless of those who try to bastardize what he stood for. No matter who attempts to tear tatters from his legacy, there are always those strongly gifted knitters of truth who stand by, eagerly ready to restore the threads that hold his legacy dear to us all.

This legacy is the type of life that we should all live. You should give a damn about your future and your children's future after you. We all should.

Laying down and taking whatever we are given has never worked, not for our generation or any generation that came before us.

The only time we had ever come out as winners were when we fought for what we believed.

It takes courage, and a willingness to give all of yourself to the cause. The strength and resolve of character that is needed for such an undertaking are almost impossible to explain.

Perhaps greater men and women than me would tell you that either you have it or you don't.

But I feel that strength is something that can be built.

How many lessons in history do we have of those who faced down weakness and built their strength brick by brick into an indestructible fortress that could not be torn down?

I like to believe that this is what I have done in my own life. By grasping on to opportunities to pull myself out of poverty, I was able to do so - but it was not easy.

It was a difficult task, one that was almost too daunting even to attempt.

But I believe that God placed a light at the end of my tunnel, a goal for which I could reach, and aspire. And as I clawed, crawled, and sometimes rolled my way to that goal post, I could feel the change that I needed in my life growing closer and closer.

Anything in our lives that is worth having, takes hard work. If you are a college man or woman, it took hard work and dedication to forge ahead even when you saw some around you, begin to fall and fail.

But if you were anything like me, you reached down deep within yourself, and you drew strength from that part of you that most people had no idea existed, and you shocked and surprised them - and sometimes you even shocked and surprised yourself. And you made it.

Well, there's your lesson. Now how will you use that strength of character to affect a change in society?

Well, first you have to be willing to confront those voices of fear inside yourself. You must be willing to lay it all on the line. It's either all or nothing. There is no in-between.

But as you mold and shape your strength into a plan, others will join you, and they will be happy to be a part of a movement that will create hope, change, and guidance for others.

I'm an example of this. When I was willing to stand against hate, I garnered support. I received letters, texts, and emails from others who supported this movement.

By using my voice, it inspired others to join in and use their voices to combat the horrors of our state's past.

The voice of the people is perhaps the strongest power in our society. After all, we are a nation with a government that is of the people, for the people, and by the people.

We must never take the voices of the people for granted. We must encourage conversation and dialogue that will drive society forward.

So this is what I did. I began to speak out against societal injustices, and I used my platform to speak against the racism in Mississippi.

As I watched the aftermath of the Mother Emanuel church massacre, I saw how Americans came together and decided that they would no longer stand for hate. I watched as the movement in South Carolina grew.

The shock of the senseless murders had galvanized Americans across the country, especially those native to South Carolina. Angry and hurt, they began to use the spotlight that was cast on them through terrible and unfortunate circumstances to amplify their voices as they spoke against injustice.

Media coverage showed how Dylann Roof, declaring himself a separatist and Nazi, often posed with the Confederate flag – the same flag that hung from state and federal buildings across the state. As more and more photos surfaced of Roof posing with the Confederate flag and Nazi symbols, South Carolinians decided that they could no longer let that flag be representative of them.

They called for the flag to come down; and eventually, their then-governor Nikki Haley listened to them, and obeyed the voices of the people.

Once South Carolina took the flag down, that makes Mississippi the last state remaining that flies a Confederate symbol over our state institutions.

Racism was thoroughly entrenched in my home state. It existed from the culture to the institution. The reality of this was almost overwhelming, but I knew the fight had to start somewhere.

The Confederate flag has been drenched with the blood of slaves. The Mississippi flag was the flag that those who championed slavery fought under in the Civil War. As they fought to continue the terrible institution of slavery, their army proudly waved this banner.

That's why I don't hesitate to tell the truth. The truth is that the Confederate symbol is a symbol of hatred, bigotry and intolerance. It's not noble. It's not righteous. And unless you are comfortable claiming that history, then you should never tell anyone that you feel this is your heritage.

Symbols of Hate

It's not heritage. It's hatred. That's as simple as I can put it. And this was why I decided to start here.

I began to use my voice to speak out against the injustices that still affect my home state. I used my position as a community leader to amplify my voice, as I spoke for many across the state who too wanted to see that flag gone.

As I said many times: If Mississippi is to ever overcome the dark history of the past, then we have to get out from under the shadow of that flag.

But this flag had been here for so long, that many were apathetic towards the tragic and horrible history that exists behind it.

I've had my critics in the past, to question why I was so adamant in taking a position on the flag. I welcome the criticism, but my answer will always be the same: After what happened in South Carolina, Mississippi became the last state to have a symbol from the Confederacy as representative of what our state stands for.

Out of 50 states, our state is the only one that thinks there's something wrong with removing a symbol that is easily equated to Nazi Germany and Hitler.

Yes, I'm serious. The Confederate flag is America's swastika. The Jewish people in Germany were murdered and terrorized by those who pushed their claims of superiority and pushed images to represent their claims such as the swastika.

That's the same thing that happened here in America with African Americans. The Confederate flag is the flag that was flown by those who wanted to keep African Americans in slavery.

Why are we still flying this flag?

Why is this even a point of contention? All of us know deep down that this is the right thing to do.

I think what astounded me the most, and still does, is Governor Phil Bryant's push back on this issue. And then to add insult to injury, the governor proudly declares "Confederate Heritage Month".

I and many activists take this as a slap in the face. In spite of all of our work to improve our home-state and make it a state that is filled with justice and love for all people, we still have to fight against a power structure that is hell-bent on maintaining the status quo.

As David fought against Goliath, now I and my fellow activists are being pitted against a governor and his fellow politicians that refuse to take down this Confederate flag, even though they recognize the damage that a Confederate flag does to this state.

Before the political leaders of South Carolina agreed to remove the flag, they faced the risk of boycott from corporations that refused to do business in a state that would let itself be used as a safe haven for racists and bigots.

Whether we realize it or not, the same thing is happening today with Mississippi.

Governor Bryant and his reckless and callous decisions are hurting this state. His refusal to advance our state into the 21st century has cost us dearly.

What company wants to seriously relocate to a state that is facing potential PR and image issues that could severely impact their business?

This is one of the reasons why we have a job crisis!

It's unfortunate, but it's true. Mississippi generally leads when it comes to poverty, education and the lack of jobs.

Why is our state among the last when it comes to these important issues?

It's because of the politicians that refuse to give the people a seat at the table. These politicians were put into office by the people; but they refuse to give voice to the issues that matter to the people.

Mississippi is not an island unto itself. In this time where so much hatred and divisiveness exists in our cultural climate, it's imperative now more than ever that our elected officials stand up and stand on the right side of justice.

I've written many columns where I express how important it is for Americans to make public stands on the right side of issues. We can't be silent when there is so much false and inflammatory rhetoric being thrown out into the wind.

We have to speak loud and ensure that the voices of justice prevail.

Governor Bryant knows what he's doing. He is relying on the apathy of Mississippians to advance his agenda of racial pride. By declaring Confederate Heritage Month, he is proudly proclaiming his love of white privilege, and he is decrying every single African American in this state.

As ineffectual as it seems to be, the governor's push back has rallied support. As he decided to dig in his heels, many of his supporters did the same.

As I observed this, I began to realize that the state would not change if the governor refused to lead by example. So I set out on a mission that would bring my words before the governor, to convince him of the error of his ways.

I wrote a letter directly to him and I published a series of columns speaking to his role in the next step of Mississippi's growth. I chose to speak to his humanness, as I wrote about America's place as the leader of the free world.

No one has ever declared our country to be wrong when our Presidents have made such declarations. So since we as Americans have placed our country as the moral authority to the world, then it is extremely important that every state in this country reflect the values of our nation.

How can the US be looked to as the bastion of liberty and justice, when there are those who still seek to demoralize a segment of our population?

As I said so many times, this isn't just a Mississippi fight. This is a fight that our entire nation must rally together and battle. The soul of America is at stake.

So as I sat down to compose my thoughts and how I would address the governor, I felt then, and I still do now, that the governor has the best interests of Mississippi at heart. The problem is that, there are currently two Mississippis.

We have an ever growing divide that separates us on racial lines, and it has created a mindset of two separate states. This is practically segregation all over again.

After the Civil Rights movement, we thought we had won this battle. We thought that America made the important changes to ensure liberty and freedom for all its citizens.

After all, how can someone oppose the concept of liberty for everyone? The only person that could and would balk at this idea, I believe, would be a truly evil individual; and I would like to think that no such person exists in my home-state.

I prefer to think of my fellow Mississippians as the best. As far as I'm concerned, we are. We have so much potential that exists in our state.

Yes, we may currently be at the bottom of many negative trends; but we can reverse this. We can change Mississippi and show the world that good prevails.

All it takes is for those who believe in the concepts of liberty and justice, to stand together.

So as I continued to use my voice to speak out against the flag, I learned that actress and Mississippi native Aunjanue Ellis was starting the "Take It Down America" movement to remove the Confederate symbol from the Mississippi state flag.

I wanted to be a part of that.

Making a difference doesn't mean that you have to be the sole person with a megaphone. Ultimately, it comes down to the chorus of voices.

One person can holler and yell for change; but when a group of people come together, there's no limit to what we can achieve.

I've witnessed activists who fell victim to an over-inflated sense of self-importance. By conflating their own selves and the issues for which they fight, some struggle to separate the two. Then it's no longer about the people and the issues. It's about the activist and their personal struggles.

If your struggle is linked with the cause that you are fighting for, then I believe that it's important to invest yourself wholly into it. Many times, this makes you fight even harder because you are more invested than someone that does not share those experiences.

But you must always be careful to not let ego and self-gratification lead you down the road of self-importance.

I always believe that there are methods of collaboration with any activist that is fighting on behalf of the people.

Ultimately the fight does not just belong to us. It belongs to everyone.

So what kind of person would I be if I refused to work with someone, just because I was not the sole organizer of an event?

That would be foolhardy, and it would eventually lead one to self-destruct.

So I reached out to Aunjanue. After she and I talked, we decided that we both had the same goal in mind, and we wanted to work together. Her idea was to take the fight out of the state to Washington, DC.

The logic was that we would be able to gather national coverage and put pressure on our legislators back home. The idea was sound, and since I was already working in DC, this made all the sense in the world to me. It was as if the stars aligned.

Aunjanue, through her name and presence, would be a media grab for this event. She had already taken a public stand on the issue when she wore a dress to the NAACP awards with the words, "Take it down Mississippi".

So she had already created a buzz. That was unique to her because not only was she an actress, but she was a television and movie star as well.

She had the perfect toolkit to grab the attention that was necessary for this event.

You see, when you are an activist and you want to make serious change in society, you have to find ways to make people pay attention to you.

Most people create a name and garner fame for themselves. This gives them the name recognition that they need so that when they march or speak out on issues, the media coverage will be sufficient enough to get the message out.

Of course, in Aunjanue's case, she was already a star and so she had the name recognition. And I really appreciated her, because she didn't have to do this. She could have been comfortably living and working somewhere else, without having to bother with the day-to-day politics of our home state.

But she decided that she wanted to be involved and that she wanted to make a difference. I knew then and there that she and I would make great working partners on any movement to help Mississippi.

I was honored when she asked me to serve as the official emcee and moderator for the event. We were joined by famed academic Michael Eric Dyson and others.

We counted the event a success because it created a national awareness about the fight in our state. And even though this fight is far from over, there have been victories along the way.

Through the work of activists such as Aunjanue, myself and many others, there have been many courageous individuals that have stood up with us to declare that Mississippi needs a new flag that is representative of all of the individuals in our state.

"One Flag for All" is an organization that has even supplied a redesign of the flag. I truly respect that kind of work, because it shows that we are not just individuals that have no plan. We want the flag to be changed, and there are those who have come together to show what that change can look like.

That display only serves to fuel the fire that rages within each of us as we continue to fight this fight against injustice and inequality.

Then there were the schools that boldly spoke out and declared that as long as the Mississippi state flag contains the Confederate symbol, then the flag would not fly at their universities.

Bold moves such as these are major milestones that make it all worth it. The fight, the struggle, the sleepless nights, the long conference calls to plan a strategy: All of this pays off in the end.

It's about remembering why you joined the fight. It's about remembering what inspired you, and what drove you to get involved in the first place.

You're not going to always receive gratitude. If you join the movement because you want fans and endless gratitude, then you're in the wrong space.

As I said before, the movement to improve the lives of all Americans requires sacrifice. It means that you have to be willing to give up your time and even be willing to make financial investments to be able to fight for the cause that you believe in.

I wish I could tell you that there's a manual for all of this. Even with this book: What I'm doing is telling my story so that it can help others who are trying to figure out how they can get involved.

But don't feel bad if your story varies from mine. There's no one way to be an activist or community leader.

In fact, it's just the opposite. Many times you face obstacles in your path, and you have to learn how to roll with the punches, and how to still achieve your goals. And through those experiences that are specific to you,

you will find the strength within yourself that will propel you forward.

You're not just fighting for yourself. Let that drive you. If the weight of the world falls on your shoulders, then use that to propel yourself ahead. If there's an obstacle in your way, use that drive to help you move it.

I would be lying to you if I told you that there are no hard times. There are always hard times; but that's okay.

I often tell people that being an activist and a community leader is not a glamorous job. It's full of hard decisions that you must make.

You will face criticism, many times from your peers. But that's how you prove your merit. If you are criticized, listen to the complaints and use it to better your position.

That's what I did. There were many who voiced their complaints about the decision that I made to speak out. It comes with the territory.

Develop a thick skin. You're going to need it. But even with the verbal barbs that I occasionally get, I wouldn't trade what I do for the world.

I'm a proud Mississippian and I credit my successes to this wonderful state. I come from Mississippi; but no matter what state you come from, you can work to improve the lives of all of your fellow citizens.

I wish you nothing but success.

Chapter 5

Confronting Issues Across the Nation

As I moved onto the national stage with published columns in USA Today, I began to address issues that affect minorities across the country. I became a warrior in the fight against racism, and I used my voice to demand justice for the 1955 murder of Emmett Till.

Working in Washington DC has given me an opportunity to advance my skill sets. As I began to find my way as a community leader and activist, I feel that my exposure in DC expanded my knowledge in ways to help push policy forward.

But one of the issues that I have struggled with as I work in Washington, DC has been remaining an active force for good in my home-state.

Mississippi is always home, no matter where I live. My mother, sisters, brother and the rest of my family are there. So I always travel back home as often as I can.

But I will be the first to admit that being in Washington so much has taken me away from the front lines, so to speak. I'm limited in the capacity that I'm able to serve my community.

But there's a flip side to that. Being in Washington, being so close to the gears that run this great country, has given me so many valuable experiences. Washington is the seat of everything that runs this nation.

I always knew there would be value in being in that kind of atmosphere. There's plenty of politics at play, but even with that, I get to have an inside look at what goes on behind the scenes.

And being in such an atmosphere that is geared towards the entire country, helped to change my outlook. For years I had been an activist with my eyes set on Mississippi and Mississippi only. But one of the things that I began to realize slowly is that change must come in Mississippi; but sometimes that change has to be driven by outside forces, much like the outside forces that prompted change in South Carolina.

So I began to think more and more on a national level. I believed that this perspective would help me to find solutions to the problems that plague us back home. As I talked with many of our lawmakers in Washington, I learned diplomacy and the importance of a network.

As I stated before, a chorus of voices is always stronger than one voice. So as I began to build my national network, I decided to tackle issues that affected Mississippi but were not necessarily specific to my home-state.

Many of the things that we talk about back home – poverty, education, healthcare – were important issues for the rest of the country. A family that lives below the poverty line, and that only has access to underfunded schools, with limited healthcare: These were the people that I felt I needed to use my voice to help.

No, I wasn't moving away from any of the positions that I had already taken. I still believe the Mississippi state flag must be changed to reflect all of the citizens of this state. I believe the Confederate symbol must be removed.

I still believe that institutional racism is a huge problem for us. But again, these problems are not specific to Mississippi.

True, there are states that don't have the issue of the Confederate flags being hoisted on their state buildings;

but many of these states are still home to racists and separatists who proudly fly that flag of intolerance as they drive down U.S. highways.

Mississippi is not experiencing anything different than what the entire country experiences.

And so I decided to use my voice to speak to all Americans. After the events of the previous year, I was better positioned to rally others to causes that would improve the lives of all.

This was an important moment for me. If you're a young activist, just starting out and trying to discover which issues you feel most strongly about, it's often intimidating to face down a city, let alone an entire nation.

That's why I encourage you to study the examples of those who went before us. I take lessons from the lives of so many, but one of the lessons that I quote the most is the example of John Lewis: "Find a way to get in the way to make noise, necessary noise, for change in our community."

If you live the life of an activist or a community leader, and you feel comfortable not speaking up against injustices, then something is wrong. This is not a time to be comfortable.

Whenever I hear that quote from Congressman Lewis, I'm reminded that I'm not supposed to get comfortable in this life. It's just the opposite. I'm supposed to make noise, make people look and listen and focus on the issue at hand.

Being in or near the spotlight of attention can be unnerving for many. But we don't do it because we love to be in that position. We do it because we love our communities and we want to create the change that we always speak about.

So I continued to make noise. I spoke on radio and television, and I wrote columns that were published in Mississippi and were even reprinted by national publications such as *USA Today*. And I began to notice that people were paying attention.

So I focused on those topics that were relevant to us as a country. As I spoke on poverty, I was able to draw from my own experiences.

This is a vulnerable space that I placed myself in. In the beginning, it was hard for me to speak on my own life. Even though I knew there were many who shared my experiences, I still felt uneasy about making myself so vulnerable.

But again, there goes that notion of comfort: I was not comfortable speaking on this topic. But I couldn't stop.

I had to continue because there were people who were depending on me. These were people who often had the same feelings that I had, except they didn't have a voice as I do. They were stuck in the cycle, unable to express to the world, the terrible things that their families face.

So they relied on me and other activists and leaders. They relied on us to give them a voice, to speak of their experiences and to make the world understand.

I knew that many were concerned about their health. As a young African American in one of the poorest counties in Mississippi, I was all too familiar with sickness. I watched as many of my friends and my own family dealt with preexisting conditions, without adequate healthcare to improve their lives.

As the healthcare fight moved to the forefront, the noise and the chatter was almost deafening. The one thing that I couldn't understand was that the concept of healthcare for all Americans was appalling to some.

I watched in shock as many states turned down the federal aid and dollars that would have poured into their states if they would work with Washington to improve the healthcare system.

I knew deep down in my heart that this was wrong, but I had never taken a public stance on healthcare. I knew that I needed to use my voice to help, but I wasn't sure that I was as informed as I needed to be to speak on this topic.

This was what prompted me to study and increase my knowledge of what President Obama was attempting to do for American citizens.

You see, there's nothing wrong with leaving your comfort zone and addressing other issues that we don't normally tackle. But you must become informed on any topic that you decide to lend your voice to.

In this day and age, we have access to so much information. Books are right at our fingertips, and many times, it's all free. So I don't believe that we have any excuse to give misinformation on whatever topic that we address.

In this information age, it's imperative that the information that we distribute be accurate and correct. If it isn't, then I'm afraid that we run the risk of doing more harm than good.

There is a Latin phrase that many doctors use: "*Primum non nocere*". It means, "First, do no harm."

I think that's a good phrase that many of us can take to heart. I joined the ranks of activism because I truly wanted to help my community. I had a fire that burned deep in me, that inspired me to dedicate my life to this cause. That same fire still burns today.

But if I ever put my community at risk, I don't think I would be able to live with myself. This is part of the great responsibility that goes along with this important job.

As I stated in Chapter 4, it's important to build a following, and even establish some fame for yourself to aid in getting out the message that you as an activist and as a community leader need to pass on to the people. But being at the forefront requires you to be vigilant and never take anything for granted.

You should always work hard to ensure that your message is accurate. Sometimes this requires that you build a team, an in-house office that serves to safeguard the cause for which you fight. After all, if your words can be invalidated, then that leaves the cause open to invalidation as well.

So first, do no harm. Take extreme care and caution to protect the reputation of those who you fight for. After all, there are many who place their faith in you. When you stand up to fight for your community, there are many who place that burden on your shoulders, and you carry their hopes and their dreams along with you on this path.

Never let them down.

So as I spoke and wrote about healthcare, I took a very public, and sometimes, unpopular stance. But again, I knew that I was right where it counted. And so I continued, never shrinking from this responsibility.

I know that there were many who appreciated the time and the effort that my team and I put into this topic. As I lectured and authored columns about healthcare, many wrote to me and expressed how they were inspired by the things that I spoke on.

That still means a great deal to me.

As I continued to stare down the topic of healthcare, I knew that I needed to address education. Even though education has always been a huge topic for the entire nation, I found myself coming right back to Mississippi to speak on the education issues that were at stake.

As many schools in Mississippi faced the reality of receiving meager funding, this threatened the school systems in many cities.

The only reason this was happening was that our lawmakers refused to make education a priority. They spoke about it and did a lot of grandstanding, but when it came time to look at actual results, there were none.

I spoke out strongly on this issue because this is an important issue to me. In my own life, I know how important education is. If I was unable to receive a quality education, then there is no way I would have ever made it to where I am now.

I watched during my years of the "Dream To Succeed" foundation as there were many young people that were hungry for education, and hungry for knowledge, just as I was. They just weren't given the opportunities by their lawmakers. The lawmakers didn't fight for them.

So where did that leave them? In the same position that I was in, struggling to climb up from the deep, dark depths of poverty.

And I will be honest: everyone doesn't have the support system that I had. If I didn't have the support of my mother and grandmother and teachers, there's no way that I could do what I do now. No way.

And that's why many of those who weren't as fortunate the way I was, still struggle to find their way out of the hole that they were born into.

This is what made me so angry. At this point in my life, I had been on both sides. I knew poverty from the inside out, and I had a great understanding of politics. This was how

I knew that if they wanted to, our lawmakers could easily turn this situation around.

But they're too focused on their polls instead of their constituents. They aren't paying attention to what matters.

This is why I spent so much time demanding a seat at the table. I didn't ask. I demanded it because it's time for those who have their finger on the pulse of the community to be allowed to talk. This is the only way we can make progress.

Perhaps the answer is not always in politics. Maybe we shouldn't wait for politicians to create a policy on their own. At least, not without them getting feedback from activists and community leaders. This would be a great way of ensuring that the interests of the people in the community are represented in the halls of the State Congress and the U.S. Congress.

But in the meantime, I couldn't stop. I took every opportunity I could to use my voice to reach everyone. I refused to get comfortable in one spot. No, there's too much work to be done.

You, as a community leader and activist, will also run into situations that you will sometimes understand better than those who govern. But I encourage you to dialogue with your lawmakers. Get them to listen to you.

Don't be afraid to voice the concerns of those who you represent. Many times when we come face to face with our council members, mayors, and governors, we feel apprehensive and are unsure. But you can't let that stop you.

Remember, there are too many depending on you. They depend on you because you can get into those spaces that they can't get into. You can get into the office of your Congressman, and you can dialogue with them and express the needs of the community.

If done correctly, this is a beautiful thing; and I truly believe that moments like these are what make our democracy work: Everyone is willing to listen to and work with everyone.

So I began to use my voice to speak on the link between poverty and education. I knew from my own experience that living in poverty could directly affect one's learning. After all, how can you focus on the words of your teacher and concentrate on the learning process when your stomach is continuously growling because your family doesn't have any food at home?

This is what causes illiteracy in low-income families; and until we find a way to break this cycle, it's going to continue.

I wrote a column to talk about this issue, and I wondered aloud why no politician had made poverty, health and literacy front and center when it's public knowledge that there are over 15 million children living in poverty in this country.

When we start facing numbers like this, then I truly believe that this is where we have to stand up and say no to political gamesmanship.

Even though I have my criticisms, I still respect the men and women who have led lives of public service and served as our lawmakers.

But if I and others don't criticize, then how will they ever know that there's a problem?

The only way our political leaders are going to take these issues seriously is when the people speak up and tell them that it's time to do something. It's time to do something about American children living in poverty. It's time to analyze the link between poverty, health, and literacy. If we're not willing to acknowledge the connection, then how are we going to work on the problem unilaterally?

So I addressed these issues. I stepped outside of my norm, and I decided to place myself before the state of Mississippi once again and now before the entire country, and speak to those things that matter to me, and others like me.

This is what you must do: You have to be willing to take on the world. If you are to be a serious change maker, then you have to put yourself all the way out there. Put it all on the line, and watch as your community reaps the benefits of your hard work and sacrifice.

So as I took on more of a position in the public eye, I learned that even though I had started to address issues that mattered to all Americans, that there were still a large number of experiences that were specific to African Americans.

It seemed that every day, we were hearing of the shootings of unarmed black men by police. I was highly alarmed at how frequent this seemed to be taking place. Once is too much, but I could understand that there are impossible situations that can happen; and although it's a tragedy, it just may not have been avoidable.

But when it happened frequently, that was evidence of an institutional problem within our country's law enforcement. And we found out that we were right when it was reported that Florida police officers were caught using the mugshots of black suspects for shooting practice.

They would literally print out the faces of individuals and place them on the shooting targets.

And these weren't even convicted criminals. They were "suspects" - which means, that they were still, by law, innocent until proven guilty. At least, they should have been. But as these police shootings showed, no one is innocent until proven guilty if you are black.

Black lives are undervalued and cheapened in our society. No one respects our lives. We have become so used to hearing of a police shooting of an unarmed African American, that it is no longer shocking to us. It's almost an everyday occurrence.

This is the result of police departments establishing a culture where black lives don't matter.

I'm sure that there have even been black police officers who were trained to see a bad person when they look at another African American. They have been brainwashed to believe that we are bad, depending on how we dress and how we walk.

This is a life-threatening precedent that has been set in our society. Perhaps the officer who shot Keith Lamont Scott in Charleston, North Carolina was required to target images of black people during his gun training. How would we know?

The good ole boy system of the police force is public knowledge. It's often talked about and parodied. Police officers have built a fraternal network where they teach each other to protect police officers at all costs and never to incriminate their fellow officer.

But what if their fellow officer is wrong? What then?

When does society stand up and address this? If we aren't even willing to acknowledge that this problem stems from the ingrained racist culture that permeates police departments across the country, and teaches them that black lives don't matter: If we aren't willing to admit this, then this problem will never go away.

Again, this is where we need our political leaders to get involved. They create the laws. Why won't they enact a study of police departments and create legislation that will save black lives?

This is on them, and this is why we need a seat at the table. You and I must start giving a damn about what happens (and doesn't happen) in congressional chambers. If our political leaders aren't willing to even address the systematic racism that exists in police departments, then we will continue to watch as more black lives are lost.

It could be me. It could be you. That's how dangerous this is. None of us are safe. And by demonizing an entire segment of the American population, we are drawing dangerous parallels to the German holocaust.

I mean, we've seen this before in history. Nothing good comes from turning a blind eye to the slaughter of people. Of course all lives matter. But all lives aren't the ones that are in danger from their police officers. It's black lives. And if you have a problem acknowledging that simple fact, then you are a part of the problem.

We know that black lives have historically been undervalued. We were classified as 3/5 of a human being during slavery, and it appears that our value has not changed. Slavery set a precedent for black lives to be considered subhuman and substandard.

Yes, I know the country has changed. I'm not arguing that. We have made tremendous progress, but there is still more progress to be made. The fight isn't over. It's far from over. And even now, we are witnessing the dangerous undercurrent of racism that exists just under the surface of our society.

We must address this. The longer we continue to kick this down the road, the more lives are at risk.

Ask yourself this question: Can you live with yourself knowing that you could have made a difference by speaking out, but you didn't? Can you look at the next hash tag, knowing that you could have been part of the movement to demand change, and you did nothing?

If it were me, I wouldn't be able to sleep at night. If I knew that I could have worked for change, I would not be okay with myself.

This is what strong activism is built on. Sometimes we don't want to look into the mirror because we're afraid of what we might see. And it's always frightening to come face to face with the realization that we just might be a part of the problem.

But this is where I'm challenging you. Don't turn away from the mirror. Keep looking; and if you see that something is wrong, then I'm challenging you to get involved.

Don't you think that you can make a difference? Dr Martin Luther King, Jr. did. When he saw great injustices taking place across America, he didn't sit down. He stood up. He decided to lend his life to this cause to improve our country.

This is what all of us must be willing to do. I talk of sacrifice. Well if Dr King was willing to sacrifice his life, then surely we must be willing to sacrifice our comfort zone and use our voices to demand change.

I don't think I'm asking too much of you. I'm asking you to fulfill your duty as an American citizen. We all have the task of doing what we can to advance our society. And if we aren't willing to do that, then I'm afraid that we are a part of the machine that is trying to hold society at a standstill.

I can't be a part of that. And if you are reading this, then I'm willing to bet that you're not willing to be a part of that either.

Well then, become proactive. Use your life to amplify the voices of those who are unable to speak for themselves.

I look at Colin Kaepernick, who literally put it all on the line because he found a cause that he believed in. He gave up his career, and he took a stand. He didn't willingly give up his career, of course. That was one of the risks that he was taking when he decided that he wasn't going to wait for the next hash tag. He decided that he would demand justice all the time.

He paid for it. But from every account that I've heard, if he had to do it all over again, he wouldn't change anything.

This is the power of finding something that you truly believe in, and are willing to fight for.

Whenever I'm able to speak to other communities about what we face, I encourage them to try to step outside of themselves.

Perhaps this would make them more empathetic to what the African American community faces.

I once wrote a column about Khadafy and Quinetta Manning, an African American couple in Madison County, Mississippi who were victimized by the police, when they had not committed any crimes.

I tried to explain to the readers that you must be willing to look at racism from outside your perspective.

You have to be willing to put yourself into the space of a black life. Only then will you truly begin to fathom what we regularly face.

In the case of the Mannings, they were accosted by the police in their own home. The police had no warrants, but they forced their way inside the Manning home and brutally attacked Khadafy while his wife watched.

This isn't an isolated story. It's one of many stories that are told not only in Mississippi but all across the country. These were the same stories that were told by our grandmothers and grandfathers during the civil rights struggle.

Well, we are in that same struggle today. Don't minimize our experiences simply because they differ from your own. One would argue that the black experience has always differed from the mainstream experiences of white people. But does that make it any less real? Of course not.

We are facing incredibly divisive times, where racism and bigotry have once again established themselves in mainstream consciousness. And until we are all willing to acknowledge this, then the problem will subsist.

I need you all to recognize that we are not so different. When I talked about healthcare, poverty, and education, these were issues that transcended racial lines. These are issues that affect us all.

So, we are not so different. We have the same concerns, the same hopes and the desire to see our families succeed. What separates us is institutional racism that has bombarded us to the point where we have to claw and fight to surpass the obstacles that are placed in front of us.

This isn't fair. If you have never been pulled over and harassed by the police, then count yourself lucky. You've never had to stare down the barrel of a policeman's gun because of the color of your skin.

But what does it say about you when you don't even care that this happens? What does that say about our society?

If you were placed in an environment where everything was stacked against you, you wouldn't be able to succeed. Then it's no wonder that African Americans are considered to be last when it comes to education and employment.

How can any community thrive when in Madison County, blacks make up 73% of arrests even though they are only 38% of the population?

Again, if we want this to change, then we have to be willing to make noise. Let's shout these statistics from the housetops. We have to force society to look in the mirror and acknowledge the terrible reality that exists for an entire segment of the American population.

I'm going to continue to use the position that I've been blessed with to fight against systemic racism, but I can't do it alone. This isn't a fight for one person or even a hundred people. If we are to create the change that we know needs to happen, then we all must get involved. We all must make that necessary noise for change.

As I continued to use my platform, I watched as the case of Emmett Till once again swept the nation by storm. Again, this is a perfect example of African Americans still dealing with the same issues that we experienced over sixty years ago.

My heart wept when it was publicized that Carolyn Bryant Donham admitted that she lied when she said that Emmett Till whistled at her and attacked her. This lie was what led to the murder of an innocent African American boy.

What Emmett, who was 14 at the time, must have thought when he realized that he would not survive the night when he was abducted from his home by three murderers. What he must have thought when he knew that he hadn't done anything wrong, but here he was facing his own mortality.

Here he was facing death at 14 years of age – over a lie.

I'm angered by this, and you should be too. Mamie Till, Emmett's mother, never got the chance to hear the truth about what took place that night. She died in 2003.

Carolyn Bryant Donham robbed Mamie Till of her son. And then she robbed Mamie Till of the truth.

Where do we as a society draw the line? Where do we make a stand and decide that this can't happen anymore?

For the past 60 years, the Till family has preached Emmett's innocence to anyone that would listen. But even now that we finally have the truth, it won't bring him back. It won't save the life that was cut short, never knowing what he had to offer the world.

We owe it to the Till family to make a stand here and now. We owe it to them to fight for Emmett and other young men and women who have been murdered over the years. We owe it to them to stand up and get involved in this fight.

Carolyn Donham is now an elderly woman, and even now after making Emmett her victim 60 years ago, she has once again victimized the Till family. I would have had so much more respect for her if she had been human enough to contact the Till family personally, and give them closure and help them heal from her cruel accusations.

But even now, she seeks to capitalize on the life of the young man whose murder she was responsible for. She's not seeking to take responsibility. It's just the opposite. She gave her testimony to an author who has placed her words under lock and key until 2036.

Until 2036!

In 2036, it will have been 81 years since Emmett was taken from his mother and his family.

So where does this leave us? In 1955, the world refused to give justice to a young black man; and in 2018, the same holds true.

Now you see why I couldn't remain silent. No matter how dangerous it was, no matter the risk, I had to stand up and fight for the Till family.

I have become good friends with members of the family. I have watched this strong family who has faced so much tragedy, still rise in the face of that defeat. I have watched them exhibit strong dignity and a powerful spirit as they continue the fight for Emmett.

Every day, I'm thankful that I was able to play a small part in helping this family, by giving my voice to this fight.

What kind of activist and community leader would I be if I remained mute on issues of justice? I must use my voice. I feel that this is what God gave me my voice for. It is to use it to fight on behalf of families across this country that have been placed in impossible circumstances and are still surviving, through an indomitable will and extreme courage.

I used my voice to hold a rally for justice – a rally for Emmett Till. I placed myself beside the Till family. Their tragedy has become my own. It should become yours too.

Only when we can truly empathize with our fellow citizens, can we spark change. By building the spirit of empathy within yourself, it forces you to place yourself in the space of others. It forces you to cry with them, to mourn with them.

When you are in that space, and that pain becomes your own, then you will be willing to do whatever is necessary to heal their hurt and their pain. You will be willing to place your life on the line as you selflessly fight for others.

This is the mark of a true activist. Yes, you will take this pain home with you. You will wake up with it. No matter what you do, you won't be able to shake the feeling of tragedy that sinks into your stomach whenever you think of that family.

But don't run from this. Embrace it. Use that tragedy to shape your thinking. Use it to embrace the life of a community activist. Use it to propel yourself forward, because when you can fight for other families as strongly as you would fight for your own, then you have made yourself into an instrument that can be used to bring change and justice for your community.

I encourage you to search deep within yourself, to push past your feelings, and embrace the feelings of others. You will find in this search that you will find yourself again – and you will be all the stronger for it. But then you won't just have your strength. You will have the strength of others.

As you stand in this space of activism, always remember that this is what it's about. It's not about you. It's not about me. It's about the people that we serve.

And I can't think of any better inspiration for my life. I hope you feel the same.

Chapter 6

The President That Gave Us Hope

After the historic presidency of Barack Obama, I am left to wonder: What's next? I tackled this question head-on while remaining hopeful, but I am also forced to consider the presidency of Donald Trump, and what this means for the future of America.

I remember the election of Barack Obama. As a young professional in 2008, I was mesmerized by his message and galvanized by his movement. In the proper context, it would be apt to say that at that moment, he became my sole inspiration.

He inspired me in ways that I didn't know that I could or even needed to be, inspired. He provided an image that gave many young African Americans something to aspire for. His calm and cool persona was just what our nation needed after enduring 8 years of war.

As a young black boy in Mississippi, sure; we had black leaders. We had black teachers, black mayors, and black congressional representatives. But even though we were well represented in our immediate areas, I never once considered it a possibility that a man who looked like me could ascend to the highest office in the world.

It's not about race – not for me. It's simply about representation. Each of us in our lives strives to reach the moment when we can place individuals in office who represent us, our culture, our beliefs and our missions. I was no different.

Wrapped in the message Barack Obama presented, was an adequate representation of my dreams and aspirations. He touched something deep within me when he spoke of hope – and he spoke of it a lot. After all, it was the central message of his campaign.

It was his mantra, and he encouraged American citizens to use it as a muse in our own lives as we dealt with the reality of the impending Great Recession.

As he took the world by storm, then-Senator Obama championed the relevancy of a concept that had not been relevant in a long time.

You recall this was after 8 years of President George W. Bush. In 2008, the country was reeling from so much. After an exhausting and seemingly never-ending war on terror, Americans were tired. We were tired of the fear that seemed to rise within each of us so soon after witnessing the horrific 911 attack in 2001.

We were tired of war, and we were tired of lies. We were tired of status quo that had been prevalent in our country for so long.

We were tired of it all.

Our country was in a period of change. Everyone was on high alert, expecting danger at every turn. Our airlines, one of the country's major traffic organs, changed their procedures at every airport in America.

Each of us was a suspect until proven guilty. The TSA, which although it is a wonderful organization that was set up to protect us, was under fire for invading the personal liberties of many through their invasive search procedures.

I understood. After such a crippling incident, everyone wanted to be safe. We have our rights, but we also have the right to be safe.

I chalk much of the outcry to public fatigue. Sure, there were incidents where TSA agents probably did abuse their power. But there were also many incidents where those same agents prevented acts of terrorism.

Americans were simply tired.

So we wanted change: The economy was in crisis. Never in a million years would I have ever thought that I would live to see the U.S. economy tailspin out of control, in ways that were eerily similar to the Great Depression of 1929. But here we were, watching helplessly as the housing market collapsed, the auto industry came close to folding, all while our military was embroiled in two wars in distant countries.

I, like many others, was shocked by these events. The country was in flux. This was what brought on the period of change: No longer could things continue on the same path. For us to survive, we had to usher in a new way.

When Senator Obama began to rise on the national scene, spouting out words such as "change" and "hope" and slogans like "yes we can," it was a welcome shift in what we had been used to seeing.

The dignity and class that he portrayed were almost a needed distraction from the economic and social perils that lurked around every corner for American citizens. And while he preached the goodwill of America, and reminded us of the pillars that uphold our great country, he did it in such a way that he did make us feel hope.

This was unprecedented for me. Never before had I witnessed a presidential candidate who addressed the issues that mattered to me. Often when I would hear him, it seemed as if he was speaking to me directly. This is how closely aligned his views were with what I, as a young American, faced with my daily struggles.

Here I was a person that came from poverty. I knew what it meant to survive on bare minimums. Often, my family didn't have enough food for us to eat. My mother could barely afford for us to live a life that was worth living – again, through no fault of her own. This is simply the stark reality that faces people who are born into poverty.

So to come from such a place of hopelessness, and then hear this man, this politician, this public figure, throw the word "hope" around so candidly was almost shocking to me – but in a good way.

Often when listening to political leaders, I felt the lack of authenticity. I could tell that their political speeches were written by others, filled with words to try to make them more appealing, but only wound up exposing the cold reality of politics.

But with Senator Obama, it was different. It was almost divine.

He showed through his actions during his campaign that he did want the best for American people. He was blessed with a passionate aura that resonated: No matter what medium you were exposed to him through, you felt the intensity of change, of hope.

This intensity, I believe, is what inspired many to come out in droves to support this great man in this historic moment.

On Election Day, there were those who had never voted before and had no intention of ever doing so. But upon hearing his message, they felt that they had to support Barack Obama.

To not support him, meant that you were on the wrong side of history; and usually, no one wants to be on the wrong side of history.

Sure, a lot of his support was crisis-driven. The economic crisis loomed over us all, and we longed to have someone in the White House, someone competent to steer the ship and correct the course of the country.

But could you blame us? Leadership is about being the captain and making those choices that will save the ship from sinking. As multiple holes popped up in the hull of America, it was of extreme importance that we placed a leader in charge that knew how to keep the ship afloat.

I watched as many of my college friends and their families lost their homes. Many of us who had recently graduated from college weren't able to find jobs in our field.

No one was hiring. How would they pay us? From day to day, no one was sure who would survive the economic disaster that was further engulfing the country with each day that passed.

We watched as companies that had been around for decades, suddenly fold.

When you see institutions that have been around since the time of your grandparents, and you watch these institutions teeter on the brink of nonexistence, it produces a panic within you.

Watching companies like Ford struggle, and seeing big banks roiled by the crisis that they helped to produce, was sobering and daunting.

So it's very understandable that many looked to the calm demeanor of a Barack Obama, and were able to find comfort in his words – enough comfort that it made them want to pledge their support to him.

For me personally, the crisis was nothing new. My life had been forged by crises.

These feelings that were alarming to everyone else were all too familiar to me. I could compare it to a person's life that was marked by trauma; and even though it has been many years, that person still has flashbacks to those ominous moments.

But having found my way out of the darkness, I knew exactly what my friends, my family, and my coworkers needed. They were in need of hope.

You see, hope was what kept my family going while we spent so many years scraping just barely to get by. As my mother worked and worked, struggling to feed her children and keep her home, it affected us tremendously.

I never knew a time when life was easy. Things always seemed to be hard for my family and me.

And when you live like this for so long, sometimes it drains the fight out of you. It drains you of all optimistic outlook because tragedy and struggle are all you've known.

But I was familiar with hope – at least a little bit. No, my family didn't sit around a table and express that we were going to rely on hope to get by.

No, that's not how it worked. It was simply a shared feeling between us. We recognized how hard things were, but we knew that it would eventually get better if we kept moving forward.

That's how hope displayed itself in my home.

So after graduating from college, I was prepared to face hardship.

As the financial crisis loomed, I applied for job after job. I lost track after my 80th try. No one was hiring. And if I, as a young and intelligent person who had been involved with social causes in my hometown, could not find work, then I knew that the situation was especially dire for others.

And as we all faced this plight together, I watched as people were mesmerized by the message that then-Senator Obama preached.

But I realized that I had to look past the message of hope that Obama provided. I needed details. I needed to know that he had a plan that would dig America out of an ever-deepening crater.

You see, politicians are trained in the use of verbiage that will appeal to a person's emotions. They know how to use words to invoke an emotional response that will hopefully garner the support of the people.

I don't think there's anything wrong with that. But we, as the people, must know how to look past that initial message and look at their plan.

And so as I looked for details, Senator Obama provided them. He released a detailed plan for recovery: An actual guideline for recovering the economic might of America through specifically tailored legislation and the firm hand of his leadership.

But even when he was talking numbers and policy and giving data, I noticed something: While providing these specifics, Senator Obama never lost the central message of his campaign, which had always been hope.

This was all I needed to know. When I decided which candidate I would vote for, I based it on one component that was important to me: I based my decision on which candidate I felt would help me and my family and my friends to be able to enjoy a good quality of life, with no stress, no fear, and no crisis.

My conscience dictated to me that Barack Obama was the one. He was the one that would foster an environment in this country that would help young Americans such as myself to obtain a career, pay back our student loans and live well.

To this day, I feel that I made the right decision.

Throughout his presidency, Barack Obama was attacked and criticized while trying to do an impossible job. But with each moment, it seemed that he exuded the same dignity and strength of character and perseverance that drew me to him in the first place.

Often, political leaders get elected to positions, and they lose that. They lose their ability to connect with the people who voted them in; and to the watchful eyes of the public, it seems that many of them change.

But this was not so with President Barack Obama. From my vantage point, he remained the same person throughout his entire presidency that he was at the beginning: He was a compassionate human being, who worked hard to ensure that America would come roaring back.

And we have. Although the beginning was dark and dreary and the light at the end of the tunnel was as faint as ever, President Obama never stopped believing in that central message of hope.

As he reeled in our Congressional representatives and garnered their support for the American Recovery and Reinvestment Act of 2009, I began not only to feel the hope. I began to see it.

Opportunities opened up before my very eyes. I was able to step into the career of my choice, an option that seemed almost impossible just a few short months before.

As I rose through the ranks of my career as a public servant, I forever feel that I am indebted to the great work that President Obama did at the very start of his presidency.

By opening up the door for me and others, he gave us the opportunity to be able to pay it forward, by sharing that same goodwill with even more of our fellow citizens.

When the President put his political credibility on the line for the Affordable Care Act, he sacrificed much to make sure that American citizens would finally get the right to have a better quality of life. This impacted families across the country, including mine.

We all have individuals in our families that have debilitating diseases. It could be one of our parents, or a sibling or a grandparent. For President Obama, it was his mother that died because she was not able to afford the best medical quality possible. Because of those that failed his mother, it drove President Obama's passion to make sure that he did not fail others.

You see, that goes back to what I mentioned in chapter 5: When you can feel the pain of your community, it gives you a power that cannot be understated. That power gives you a laser-sharp focus because you know what others feel.

In President Obama's case, he knew what it was like to watch as his mother fall sick, and eventually succumbed to her disease. That incredible pain that he felt spurred him on as he fought for every American citizen, giving us his all to ensure that we don't have to go through what he and his family endured.

And after the Affordable Care Act was passed, millions of Americans gained access to medical care that prolonged, and in many cases, saved lives. We had the opportunities that President Obama's family did not have, and I will forever thank him for what he did to save American lives.

When people say the word "hero", he comes to my mind. This man has been my hero.

Some of my classmates who had always dreamed of serving our country were serving in the two wars in the Middle East region, which seemed to become more dangerous every day.

I won't talk about my politics of the Iraq and Afghanistan wars; but no matter what, I have always supported our troops. My career was sparked by my desire to fight for those who had fought for us.

If these Americans could be so brave to be willing to put their lives on the line for America, then we needed to be just as brave to put ourselves on the line to fight hard to protect their rights.

I have always felt that this is one of the major beliefs that President Obama and I share. He made the promise during his campaign that he would end the wars in Iraq and Afghanistan, which had devolved into conflicts of "bottomless hole" proportions.

There was no end in sight. With our troops on the ground in the Middle East with no clear-cut goal post for victory, it was a potential catastrophe which could only result in the loss of even more lives.

President Obama, through his unique vision, recognized this; and he brought our soldiers home. He brought them back where they could still serve the country that they love, but on a much safer battlefield.

But although the President moved to end our foreign occupations, he never forgot his duty to obtain justice for our country.

When someone attacks American citizens, then they have to answer for their crimes.

Thanks to President Obama, Osama Bin Laden was made to answer for his crimes against the United States of America - and not only him, but others in terrorist organizations who engaged in plots to try to destroy us.

President Obama truly kept America safe during his presidency.

But he wasn't only a strong leader for Americans. Obama was a strong leader for the world. Many countries were as enamored of him as we have been, for they look to that same strength of character that inspires us here, to inspire them in their nations.

Our President was almost treated like a rock star when he visited foreign countries. And while he was indeed strong, he tempered his strength with the same compassion that I had witnessed during his campaign; and as he toured the world on behalf of America, he single-handedly improved the reputation and standing of our country, and restored us as the leading nation of the free world.

There's so much that Obama did for this country, and for the world, but one issue that greatly matters to me was when he took a stand for the LGBTQ community and championed the rights of Americans to love whoever we choose to.

This was an unprecedented moment of progress. Never before had any president taken what was called a "liberal" approach to a very real issue that impacted so many American citizens. But to me, it wasn't liberal. It was simply the right thing to do.

The American dream has been restored, regardless of what many want to convince themselves of now. President Obama was the instrument that renewed the American spirit within us all.

But where does that leave us now? After the ascension of Donald Trump to the presidency, many of us have become disillusioned as we watch him attempt to roll back every single marker of progress that was established by the Obama administration.

Where President Obama gave us hope, it seems that President Trump's mission has been to dash those same hopes. I know there are many that would disagree, but I am sure that even the largest skeptic would agree with me that President Trump's goals are not geared towards helping young Americans – especially those of color.

Where Barack Obama's presidency preached the message of a more united nation, Donald Trump's presidency has consistently attempted to widen the divides that separate us more now than ever before. Barack Obama kept his promises, and it seems that Donald Trump intends to keep his as well.

During his campaign, President Trump repeatedly assured his supporters, many of whom are bigoted, racist and misogynistic, that he would work to empower them and take away the power from "the others". Those "others" largely being anyone who isn't white, isn't Christian, and isn't straight. And he has done just that.

I've watched, almost horrified, as President Trump has once again demoted the status of America to the world. With President Obama, we took 100 steps forward, but just in the first year of Donald Trump's presidency, it seems that we have taken 1,000 steps backwards.

The fervor with which President Trump fights to strip away rights from Americans is unprecedented and nearly beyond belief. After witnessing the historic elections of 2008 and 2012, it never once occurred to me that we would face another historic election in 2016 – but one that was geared towards disadvantaging American citizens rather than fighting for them.

Many of us still struggle to understand what we are currently facing. Where our world was once bigger,

President Trump seeks to limit us and our horizons by restricting freedoms and removing liberties.

The danger that lies in this cannot be overstated. I won't speak on the dark cloud that surrounds his election, as I believe in the American justice system and its ability to discover the truth. So giving voice to my suspicions is not necessary at this time. But even without mentioning this very concerning issue, there are so many others concerning issues to which I could devote a full book.

As pundits debate the validity of a Trump presidency, I believe it's too easy to take our eye off the ball and lose sight of the fact that we must all be willing to fight for our rights.

Many of us are too silent. We sit idly by, and we know that our rights are being stripped; but instead of making noise and making our voices heard, we do nothing.

This is not the time to be silent. This is not the time to be apathetic. If there was ever a time to fight, this is it - right now, at this moment. And we're not just fighting for ourselves.

We're fighting for the future and the soul of our country. We fought just recently. President Obama was able to galvanize the masses around the concept of hope, and the idea that to create change, we would have to fight for it.

So this is not some far-off concept that I'm writing about right now. This is the legacy of the free citizens of America.

If we don't fight, the damage that is being done to America could become irreversible - if we don't push back against what we know is wrong.

There's an old saying by Edmund Burkes: "The only thing necessary for the triumph of evil is for good men to do nothing."

As Donald Trump toys with the nuclear arsenal of our country, inviting and seeking to provoke conflict that could potentially cost millions of lives, we cannot afford to do nothing. The irresponsible behavior of this president is dangerous to every American citizen.

When he recklessly engages in Twitter dialogue about nuclear holocaust, it's almost as if he is holding a loaded gun to the head of every American. This is how dangerous talk of nuclear war is.

Where are our good citizens, that will take action and speak out against the immature and reckless behavior of our president?

It's not too late, but the harsh truth is that we should have never stopped using our voices to speak out against the harmful effects of a Trump presidency.

During his campaign, he touted the most divisive message that I have ever been a witness to. The dangerous rhetoric during his campaign emboldened fringe racist groups and inspired them to come out and take a public role in American society.

Now where once these groups were on the fringe and were outliers of civilized society, they have now gone mainstream, with the tacit support of the President of the United States.

White supremacist leaders such as former Ku Klux Klan leader David Duke have routinely voiced their support and approval of President Trump. They feel that his goals align with their own, as they seek to expunge anyone who is not white from American society.

This has got to be the driving force behind President Trump's desire to remove Hispanic Americans from the country. When he campaigned on the promise of building a wall between America and Mexico, his supporters cheered and gave deafening applause.

Although he has not delivered on his campaign promise to build that wall, that doesn't make the rhetoric that he espoused any less dangerous. After all, the President sets the tone for the public discourse of the country. And while President Obama set the tone of hope, President

Trump has, it seems, firmly established a xenophobic tone of intolerance.

The President doesn't try to hide his seeming hatred for African Americans and Hispanic Americans. When white supremacists descended on Charlottesville, Virginia with a march to support their white privilege, President Trump outright refused to condemn them. Even when their march of hate brought chaos, confusion and even death, President Trump still refused to condemn these racist individuals.

So we know where he stands. He makes no secret of it.

And if he is bold enough to express his hatred of anyone who is not white candidly, then surely we can be bold enough to express that what he is doing, isn't right. It's wrong.

In school, I remember reading about historical events that shaped the direction of the country: events such as the 1963 March on Washington for civil rights, which was organized with the help of someone that I consider a mentor: Congressman John Lewis.

John Lewis is considered a bastion of the civil rights movement, an iconic figure who passionately fought for what he believed in to change the system; and then once that system changed, he became a part of the system to help usher in change for the rest of the country.

To see President Trump deliver insults and barbs to such an esteemed member of the community will forever be an insult of the highest magnitude. While Donald Trump was building his empire on the backs of illegal immigrants, John Lewis was fighting for civil rights for African Americans. And also for those immigrants—for if he was able to knock down the barriers that blocked achievement for African Americans, then that meant that the way was now clear for everyone else too.

But to Donald Trump, this means nothing.

President Trump is the epitome of racism, xenophobia, homophobia, and misogyny. He seems to revel in being the poster child for everything that is truly wrong with our country.

So where can he possibly lead us, but to an even darker path littered with mangled shadows that threaten to pull us even deeper into the abyss?

This is why it is so important for us to become actively engaged within our communities to comeback this dark side of American history. We have made great strides in America. President Barack Obama and First Lady Michelle Obama are great examples of Americans who understand the importance of progress and change. We cannot lose this concept of progress and change because this is what

America was found upon. Hope gives us the ability to continue to dream and envision a greater day for our country but this hope is only a reality with action by you, the American people. Let's not every forget that America is still a democratic society.

Chapter 7

My Truth Gave Me My Voice

For 30 years, I spent my life not standing in my complete truth. I allowed my Southern roots along with public opinion cultivate my truth instead of finding my own voice. By standing in my truth, I found my voice.

I spent the first half of my life in my home state of Mississippi, where I attended college, started a career and began my work as a public servant. My voice was cultivated by religious views and status quo. It was not until the governor of Mississippi and lawmakers attempted to put in place House Bill 1523, a bill that allows discrimination against the LGBTQ community based on their sexuality that I realized it was time for me to speak up.

I will never forget I was home in Mississippi receiving the Top 50 under 40 Award from the Mississippi Business

Journal when the governor and lawmakers placed this bill on the House floor.

I received a message from a young man who said his mother looked up to me but hated him for being gay. I then realized it was vital for me to stand in my truth even more.

I released a letter to my fellow LGBTQ family in my home state of Mississippi. In this letter, I talked about my lack of support and speaking out on behalf of the LGBTQ community and using my platform to support and help fight discrimination. This step to stand in my truth was very scary, and I thought I would lose everything I had worked so hard for over the course of my 30 years on this earth. Indeed, that happened. I lost speaking engagements across the South, and many distanced themselves from my company.

As a result, I began the journey of finding my voice within my truth in 2017. I began to find strength and a sense of boldness to speak up and speak out like never before. On this journey, I started to speak up louder in regards to the Confederate emblem on the Mississippi flag, health care, racial reconciliation, poverty, education, economic development, Emmett Till, and helping to educate citizens across the South on how crucial it is to speak up and hold political leaders accountable.

My Truth Gave Me My Voice

The most powerful moment in 2017, was when I organized and planned the Emmett Till Rally. This moment was when my voice came full circle. I heard the news of Carolyn Bryant Donham, the woman who claimed Emmett Till whistled at her and attacked her, had admitted she lied. I spent a few weeks after hearing this news battling with the idea of how could I use my platform to speak out against this injustice.

I started by researching the case, speaking with activists and other organizations. After doing all my research, I found that so many were OK with staying quiet. At that moment, I was quickly reminded of Congressman John Lewis' words to me: "When you see injustice within your community, speak up, speak out, find a way to get in the way and make some noise for change."

As a result, I planned and organized the Emmett Till Rally demanding justice and an apology for the lie of Donham that led to the murder of Emmett Till. At this moment, I learned the power of using your voice for change, ignoring the negative noise that comes with the territory of initiating change within your community. I also found the depth of my voice and how important it is always to step up and make noise when you see injustice.

Today, I want to encourage others to speak up. True change-makers don't get discouraged with noise and distractions. Remember this: We must never stop speaking up against injustices within our community. What if civil right activists like Martin Luther King Jr and John Lewis had stopped speaking up against injustices? Would we have seen a Barack Obama? Keep speaking truth to power.

If you truly want to give a damn and become the change that you want to see, then there are no shortages of causes to fight for.

Throughout this book, I have attempted to give you a look into my past, my present and my future, so that you would hopefully see why I had to get involved. When there is so much that needs to change, then what kind of person would I be if I decided that I didn't need to make a difference?

We all must work hard to make a difference. It starts by giving a damn about your community, about your city, your state, and finally the entire nation.

As I said before, your journey won't be the same as mine. But hopefully, your drive and your fervor to work hard for what you believe in will mirror what I hope I have shown to the world.

I always hope that I have been a good example of activism and community leadership because ultimately, I want to help mold the next generation that is coming up behind me and that are working their way into the space where they will take on the responsibility of being a voice for their community.

I truly believe that there is no greater purpose for my life, than my calling to help others.

Yes, it's hard, and it's difficult; but when you see the results of your hard work and you see the positive changes that have resulted from what you do, and then you will find satisfaction that is immeasurable.

So step forward. As the saying goes, be the change that you want to see. And as you step forward, watch as others step with you.

Many times, as we make a bold step, it emboldens others to step right along with us and to be the support that we need to make a difference.

So I thank you for reading this book about my journey, and I look forward to working with you to make the world a better place.

ABOUT THE AUTHOR

Duvalier is a political columnist, motivational speaker, community activist and CEO of Duvalier Malone Enterprises. His work places him squarely on the front lines regarding the issues of equal rights and equal opportunities for all. When people want action, they call Duvalier Malone. His work has been featured in USA Today, News One, and ABC.

You can follow Duvalier Malone at:

duvaliermalone.com • Facebook.com/duvaliermaloneofficial • Twitter: @duvaliermalone

Instagram: @duvaliermaloneofficial

LinkedIn: @duvaliermalone

Made in the USA
Middletown, DE
24 February 2021